"It seems that in the twenty-first century, more and more people are spending their lives in isolation from each other—not the isolation that comes from living alone, though this seems to be a growing problem in some societies, but the isolation that is the result of creating artificial barriers between ourselves and others.

"Koshin Paley Ellison has written a manual for personal growth and change based on a contemporary interpretation of Buddhist refuge and precepts, making it accessible to everyone, not just those interested in or practicing Buddhism. Using anecdotes, quotes, and reflective questioning, he prompts us to become aware of the barriers we have erected around ourselves and suggests ways by which we can dismantle them. His message is one of hope: that through personal transformation we can develop courage, openheartedness, and compassion in our relationships with others, and enrich our own lives."

—His Holiness the 17th Karmapa, Ogyen Trinley Dorje

T0024480

"I am so grateful for the light Koshin brings to the world. His wisdom teachings in *Wholehearted* will transform your heart, mind, and soul."
—Donna Karan, fashion designer and founder of the Urban Zen Foundation

"It is difficult to be honest and simple, and in today's world it is so necessary and healing. Koshin uses the Buddhist precepts to stay real and available, which makes his writing valuable and crucial. His commitment to transparency makes it possible for me to show up as my true self so that pure communication is exposed as the recipe for being alive and joyful."
—Rodney Yee, yoga teacher and author of *Moving Toward Balance*

"Koshin Paley Ellison shares his extraordinary compassion and bright wisdom with pithy advice that can help any of us cultivate a richer and more nourishing life. *Wholehearted* gives a vibrant wake-up call from a Zen mensch."
—Daniel Goleman, coauthor of *Altered Traits*

"Koshin Paley Ellison writes with authenticity, vulnerability, and depth. In *Wholehearted*, he prescribes connection, inspiration, and love to heal us as individuals and as a society. I consider this very good medicine."
—Dr. Andrew Weil, founder of the University of Arizona Center for Integrative Medicine and author of *8 Weeks to Optimal Health*

"The subtitle of this wonderful book says it all: *Slow Down, Help Out, Wake Up*. In a writing style that is elegant and eminently readable, Koshin Paley Ellison illuminates a path of connection, care, and love. The depth of his experience as a Zen teacher and practitioner reveals itself throughout this work, showing us how to live a wholehearted life."
—Joseph Goldstein, author of *Mindfulness*

"*Wholehearted* is full of nuance, humor, and tenderness. I found it such a useful guide to the profound teachings, and it left me with lots to think about and to try to activate in my own life."
—Laurie Anderson, avant-garde artist, composer, musician, and film director

"In *Wholehearted*, Koshin Paley Ellison offers his personable and creative approach to the precepts, making it clear that compassion and unselfish caring are at the heart of Zen."
—Norman Fischer, poet, senior Zen priest, and author of *The World Could Be Otherwise*

"This jewel of a book is packed with inspiring and timeless wisdom, pointing us toward freedom. Practical and delightful, each page is nourishing, leaving you more tender and more connected to humanity. This is a book for everyone."
—Ruth King, author of *Mindful of Race*

"To meet Koshin is like being embraced by hope. This book is like having the best long-lunch conversation ever, where you leave with a new best friend. I love Koshin and now I can take him with me wherever I go."
—Anthony Edwards, actor and director, winner of a Golden Globe and six Screen Actors Guild Awards

"With examples from personal experiences that reveal his unpretentious humanity and good-natured humor, Koshin makes the ancient wisdom of Zen feel intuitive for our contemporary minds."

—Ira Byock, MD, author of *Dying Well* and *The Best Care Possible*, Geisel School of Medicine at Dartmouth

"Koshin writes with the clarity of a bell. From everyday moments he takes timeless wisdom. With elegant language he blesses ordinary annoyances with breath and insight. And with simplicity he uncovers the complex heart of human stories."

—Pádraig Ó Tuama, poet and theologian, author of *In the Shelter*

"A kind guide for meeting life's challenges with more equanimity, resilience, and compassion."

—Frank Ostaseski, author of *The Five Invitations*

"*Wholehearted* is wonderful guidance for the sixteen bodhisattva precepts written by an American Zen teacher for American people. An excellent work to make the Dharma available for people living in the modern society."

—Shohaku Okumura, Roshi, author of *Living by Vow*

"Koshin Paley Ellison, a monk living in New York City, reinterprets the timeless teachings of Zen Buddhism in a contemporary way that is conversational, insightful, and unexpectedly irreverent!"

—Shakil Choudhury, author of *Deep Diversity*

"There are SO many books about Zen and Buddhism. This is one I would recommend."

—Jan Chozen Bays, Roshi, MD, teacher at Zen Community of Oregon, and author of *Mindfulness on the Go* and *Mindful Eating*

"Although the book is serious in content, Koshin's lightheartedness shines through. Precepts do not have to be a heavy subject, but can be viewed as joyful guiding lights, as Koshin demonstrates."

—Gerry Shishin Wick, Roshi, abbot of Great Mountain Zen Center and coauthor of *The Book of Equanimity*

"Readers will find the nourishing sustenance of wisdom and kindness in this excellent rendering of the Zen Buddhist precepts."

—Egyoku Nakao, Roshi, abbot of the Zen Center of Los Angeles

WHOLEHEARTED

Slow Down, Help Out, Wake Up

Koshin Paley Ellison

Edited by Emma Varvaloucas

Wisdom Publications
199 Elm Street
Somerville, MA 02144 USA
wisdompubs.org

Library of Congress Cataloging-in-Publication Data
Names: Paley Ellison, Koshin, author. | Varvaloucas, Emma, editor.
Title: Wholehearted: slow down, help out, wake up / Koshin Paley Ellison; edited by Emma Varvaloucas.
Description: Somerville, MA: Wisdom Publications, [2019] |
Identifiers: LCCN 2018039808 (print) | LCCN 2019000056 (ebook) | ISBN 9781614295495 (e-book) | ISBN 9781614295259 (pbk.: alk. paper) | ISBN 9781614295495 (ebook)
Subjects: LCSH: Sotoshu—Doctrines. | Buddhist precepts. | Religious life—Sotoshu. | Spiritual life—Sotoshu.

ISBN 978-1-61429-525-9   ebook ISBN 978-1-61429-549-5

23 22 21 20 19   5 4 3 2 1

The illustration on page 175 is courtesy of Taisan Tanaka. Cover design by Philip Pascuzzo. Interior design by Tony Lulek. Set in Arno Pro 11.5/16 pt.

"Dervish at the Door" by Rumi was translated by Coleman Barks and is used courtesy of the translator.

Wisdom Publications' books are printed on acid-free paper and meet the guidelines for permanence and durability of the Production Guidelines for Book Longevity of the Council on Library Resources.

✿ This book was produced with environmental mindfulness. For more information, please visit wisdompubs.org/wisdom-environment.

Printed in the United States of America.

Please visit fscus.org.

Table of Contents

For Chodo
and
the New York Zen Center
for Contemplative Care sangha

Ichi-go ichi-e.

One moment, one chance.

Introduction:
Waking Up from Zombieland

I am a Zen Buddhist monk. I have a shaved head. I wear a lot of black, and I have a habit of talking about how awesome meditation is. Basically, I'm Mr. Miyagi—that's what the deli guys downstairs from our Zen Center call me, anyway.

With my husband, Chodo, I cofounded a non-profit organization, the New York Zen Center for Contemplative Care; it's in the heart of Chelsea, New York City, if you ever want to visit. The Zen Center offers guidance for people in meditation, trains medical professionals and other folks in compassionate caregiving, supports people and their loved ones through serious illness and death, and assists family and friends during their grieving process. There's no karate, though.

I actually wanted to be a Zen monk since I was a kid, which I admit is perhaps rather unusual. I saw a photograph of one in a magazine when I was eight years old. He was standing in the middle of Tokyo wearing his *ajirogasa* hat, which is this massive woven bamboo hat that looks like an overturned bowl, and his black monk's robes. Blurred figures in suits were all scurrying to and fro around him; he stood in the center, the only one in focus. I remember saying to my grandfather, "That's what I want to be." It was something about his stillness—or it might've been the amazing hat.

My family had been deeply affected by the Holocaust, and I grew up with relatives who were living with a lot of unprocessed trauma, which manifested itself as verbal, physical, and sexual violence. Being gay opened me up to my own suffering at the hands of my peers. On school mornings and at the end of the day, the school bully would be waiting for me at the bus stop, and once again I would have to run the gauntlet. In hindsight this is probably why I gravitated toward the calm energy of the monk.

When I eventually became a monk, I realized just how much healing I had to do. When I left my family home, I had great difficulty trusting others; I was living with a lot of hurt. I felt very sure that all the bad things that had happened to me gave me license to live my life with a certain entitlement. And because I was afraid of how I might be further hurt if I let people in, I built an elaborate wall around myself, which I would never allow anyone to climb over, because I didn't want anyone to find out how sad I was. Even when I was introduced to Buddhism, I thought of myself as the consummate outsider, never to love or to be loved. I got into it, actually. It was my thing.

At age eighteen, I was on a bus in Colorado, and a warm-faced woman struck up a conversation with me. I had started practicing Buddhism by then, and she had too, so she asked me which community I was affiliated with. I responded, "I have a lot of teachers—Daido Loori Roshi, Jack Kornfield, Sharon Salzberg . . . but I don't practice with any one community in particular."

"Oh," she said. "So you're a lone wolf."

"Yes!" I nodded and smiled.

She went on, "You know what's interesting about lone wolves? They're sick. Wolves are pack animals, and they often mate for life. So if you see a wolf by itself, there's actually something wrong with it."

I will always remember being on that bus, its funky Greyhound smells all around me, and being totally struck dumb by her comment.

Holy shit.

I share this with you because what I was suffering from—the "lone wolf phenomenon"—is a common characteristic in our society today. Our own personal, emotional habits of isolation have now become part of the culture itself. This is how bad it has gotten: a recent study surveyed incoming college freshmen about their greatest fear around entering college; the answer was interacting with other people—which is supposed to be one of the most basic human behaviors!

I'm sure a sociologist could give you a thorough

and nuanced explanation of all the factors that have contributed to these cultural habits. (The popularity of smartphones comes to my mind.) But regardless of the reasons, I see it often in my students as a Zen teacher and in my patients as a chaplain. People are afraid of looking at and being with each other. They're afraid of—and paradoxically long for—honest, loving, and ordinary conversation. There's an incredible amount of awkwardness and odds are, in the coming generations, it's going to get worse. Odds are, too, if you're reading this book, you've felt—acutely—the heavy weight of isolation yourself. It can be extraordinarily painful.

At the movies and streaming on our devices are images of robots and zombies taking over the world. We love a good apocalypse flick in which humanity is besieged by enormous AI machines or the walking dead. But look at the way people sit in restaurants or walk to their car or train: head down, face closed, walls up. The zombies are here, and they are us. Desperately hungry for connection, lost in the narratives we've constructed

about the past and the future, we look to our
phones and computers for a morsel of false comfort, or we convince ourselves that someone else's
life will bring us contentment or authenticity. I
see the zombies everywhere, even in my own mir-
ror. How do we wake up from Zombieland?

Recently, at my gym, a guy I see all the time
but had never spoken to was in the locker room
at the same time as me. I had always thought him
to be a little pretentious; he was never friendly to
anyone—he never made eye contact or smiled or
struck up conversation. He usually used a locker
far away from mine, but that day he was adjacent
to me, and he had his arm in a sling. "What happened?" I asked.

When he turned to answer me, he had tears in
his eyes. He had suffered a compound fracture in
his collarbone, he told me, and as we got to talking
he shared that right after he hurt his collarbone,
his mother had gone to the hospital and suddenly
died. He was in so much physical and emotional
pain, but he was also so surprised and happy that

someone was talking to him about it. As for me, it made me reflect on how much distance I had created between myself and another human being just by making up a story in my head about who this person was. I'd done this for *two years*. When I finally spoke to him, he wasn't pretentious at all. Just shy, tender, and sad.

This is what this book is about: reversing our isolation by coming to know the emotional patterns that keep us trapped in our own heads, and learning how to be in relationship again. Or, in other words, it's about bringing connection and care into your life in a very real way. Not an easy task! But we're in it together—all of us zombies and lone wolves.

You already know I'm a Zen monk, so it probably won't surprise you that what I have to say about this comes mainly from the Zen tradition, although I've also been known to recap a favorite fairy tale or two. If you're not a Buddhist, though, don't worry; this book is about getting in touch with your own values, whether those come from a spiritual tradition or another source that you hold close to your heart, so you can live energetically, authentically, and lovingly. The method I'm using to help you do this in Zen is called the sixteen precepts, but I'll use that term "precept" sparingly. It often calls to mind a series of strict commandments that you must follow lest you be struck down by lightning. So for our purposes, it's better to understand them as prompts for investigating your own life—how you're causing yourself and others pain, and how you might mitigate that pain.

You'll notice a few reoccurring themes throughout this book. The first is paying attention. Zen people put a lot of stock in paying attention, which is actually pretty hard to do, especially when what you're currently paying attention to kind of sucks (more on that later!). Their technique for building up the paying-attention muscle is meditation; this is the sitting, eyes gazing down, soft and upright pose you've likely seen before, although, if I'm being truthful, meditation isn't all that chill. You can choose to try meditating if you'd like (basic instructions are in the back of this book), but you can also practice paying attention while just going about your day-to-day routine. This is one of the ways we start to reestablish connections with others. It also provides a solid ground from which to investigate our own behavior, because you're certainly not going to be able to enact meaningful change if you're walking around unaware of what's going on around you.

The second is service. I like to sum this one up as "your life isn't (only) about you." What a relief! Because, man, wouldn't it be a struggle if it were? One of my favorite quotes ever is by this old Japanese teacher named Kobo Daishi. He was a radical who devoted his life to bringing Buddhism to the masses back when it had been reserved as an elitist activity for the clergy. He said that you can tell the depth of someone's enlightenment by how they serve others. Dr. Martin Luther King Jr. agreed: he said that what you do for others is life's most persistent and urgent question. I'm not saying you need to go volunteer in a soup kitchen, although formally volunteering is certainly an activity worth considering. I'm pointing more to service on an ordinary level. How do you treat your neighbor, your sister, the lady sitting next to you at the coffee shop? What would life be like if you were—even just a little—less interested in your own stories, problems, opinions, and so on and more interested in what's going on with the people around you?

Recently I was reading that one of the most popular burial choices right now is to seal your grave so that no water can get inside to disturb your dead, rotting body. One funeral director I met told me, "That way, you'll know your loved ones will be safe." In many ways, we live like this: sealing ourselves off from each other. Sometimes we even die like that. But it's a false sense of safety, living from inside a coffin. It might seem paradoxical, but instead of contracting inward, try expanding outward, and take the world around you into account. It's far more freeing. This is how I understand service.

The third is nonseparation, or intimacy. There's another old Japanese teacher who I like a lot: Dogen. He wrote in one of his many texts, "The wholehearted practice of the Way that I'm talking about allows all things to exist in enlightenment and enables us to practice one seamless reality in the path of emancipation. When we go beyond the barrier and drop off all limitations, we are no longer concerned with conceptual distinctions." Sounds highfalutin, I know. Dogen tends to sound like that. You can think about that quote like this: You're never going to get out of interacting with other people—and if you do, it's most certainly a cause for concern—so you might as well learn how to do it. This inescapable connection is what Dogen means by "one seamless reality." It's an invitation to collapse the gaps we create between us—those many gaps we make in so many ways. For me, truly realizing that we're all in it together, the only sensible response is to live a life of generosity and love.

How to Read This Book

This book is about how to live the life of an awakening being, sometimes called a *bodhisattva* or a *mensch*, someone who cares for others in all of the many ways that care can manifest. This person may serve by being engaged with an ethical livelihood, reconciling the divided, feeling joy for the celebrations of others, cultivating partnerships with the suffering, seeing occasions for showing gratitude to others who have helped them, treating all they encounter with respect, and sitting with frightened beings in the midst of fear.

Living in this way brings us out of isolation and into a relationship with the world and its inhabitants that is full and vibrant.

This book is organized traditionally, but these guidelines and this practice are for everybody. In this book, I give one chapter for each precept. The subtitles of the chapters give the more traditional formulation of the precept, but the chapter title expresses the way I want to open it up to you— show you perhaps how to approach it and embrace it and integrate it.

First are the three treasures, or refuges. These are essential aspects of a life of attention, care, and love. They are the oldest of the sixteen, as they were formed by the first people who studied with the historical Buddha, the guy who mapped this path and taught it to others. Traditionally, the refuges were meant to be deeply appreciated. They are comprised of the awakened mind, the teachings, and the community of practitioners; I introduce them in this book as a commitment to wakefulness, receptivity of life, and being in community. Only when these three are integrated can we truly support moving the needle of transformation. Next, the three pure precepts are built on the three treasures. Traditionally, they are ceasing from evil, doing good, and doing good for others. Sounds like a tall order! Yes, *good* and *evil*, and yet perhaps not how you usually think of them. Essentially, they are how to cultivate a mind open to possibility, how to remain open to everything the world holds, and how to act from love. The first six precepts give us a strong foundation to work with the final ten precepts, which examine carefully and specifically how to orient our lives.

You can certainly go in order, reading the book

from front to back, but you don't necessarily have to. Each precept is represented by a short reflection, which stands on its own as a prompt for consideration. Each is a chance to contemplate what that topic means for you in your own life. It's like a navigational tool: what direction is my life going now, and where do I want it to be going? So feel free to flip to any reflection that grabs you, and work with it for however long it suits. That could mean for the next hour, the next week, the next year—or more. But don't feel that you need to take them on all at once. They're meant to be returned to, again and again, and their lessons overlap and reflect one another, like the many facets of a single jewel.

I have included a couple of contemplations to engage with each precept. These are questions that I like to explore when considering how to work with a precept—but they're not questions to solve or answer. They are meant to be contemplated. In the old myth of Oedipus and the sphinx, Oedipus thought he had to solve the sphinx's riddle, but when he did (and what a clever person he thought he was!), the sphinx died, and Oedipus's life went to shit. What I mean to say is this: Keep the question in front of you. There's no need to solve it. Just be in relationship with it.

There are a few things to keep in mind as you begin to work with the precepts. The first is that they're not meant to be a destination. They're more like the North Star—you travel toward it, but you never arrive. There's no state of perfection to achieve, no perfect person to become. If there is a goal, it is to rest in being perfectly imperfect. So if some of the precepts are more difficult for you than others, it's all right. Don't beat yourself up, and remember that a life of love includes you in that love, too.

The second might be best illustrated by a story. I have a student named Claire who was involved in a biosphere project where scientists created their own miniature world. It was the size of three football fields, and they brought in forest and lakes and marsh and desert, 3,800 species of animals, and eight humans beings. One striking thing about this biosphere, Claire told me, was that the trees didn't do well at all. They wouldn't grow straight. The scientists found that it was because there was no resistance in the biosphere: no storms, no winds, no extremes of temperature, which are the things that strengthen the heartwood of the tree, that give it its resilience. We can practice developing heartwood through being fully alive in the winds of life.

There's no use pretending that life isn't hard sometimes. But it's also wonderful and amazing and a million other things. This book is about embracing those countless qualities. You don't need to be happy about all the bad things life contains, and you don't need to solely identify with them, either. Even the worst situations may have beneficial outcomes, if you wait long enough to see them arise. So much depends on our ability to hold both a wide and focused view together. The key thing to remember, especially when you encounter difficulties with enacting these precepts in your life, is this: keep going.

I want to tell you one more story. One of the most beloved figures in my life was my grandma, Mimi, who on her deathbed taught me how to love in the way I hope this book teaches you. I was one of her primary caregivers in the last five years of her life. I was staying with her in the hospice when she was actively dying, and one night she woke me up in the middle of the night shouting, "Wake up. Wake up." I was immediately upright. She was crying when she said, "I'm so sorry."

"For what?" I asked.

"I didn't know until this moment what it meant to truly love you," she responded. This was quite startling to me, because I had never felt so loved in my whole life. I felt adored by her—and adoring of her. But she had never quite gotten the Buddhist monk situation, and she told me that a part of her had contracted away from me because of it. "Only now as I'm dying," she said, "do I understand what loving really means. It means to love all the things about someone, even the things that frighten you or that you don't understand." During her time in hospice, many of my Zen friends had visited with her, just to hang out—to sing a song or give her a pedicure or eat a sandwich or whatever. I wonder if that helped her warm up to my Zen path and bring her to this revelation.

And then she suggested that Chodo and I create a nonprofit organization that would train people how to take care of others and teach people about "the Zen." So the New York Zen Center for Contemplative Care—an integration of my whole life's work (poetry, caregiving, Zen practice, teaching, and love)—was founded by Mimi Schwartz, this four-foot-nine Jewish immigrant woman from Brooklyn. It was her idea, which came out of her experience of being loved and loving in return.

This is the work we have ahead of us in this book. The reward is life itself.

For me, forgiveness and compassion are always linked: how do we hold people accountable for wrongdoing and yet at the same time remain in touch with their humanity enough to believe in their capacity to be transformed?

—*bell hooks*

Part I   The Essentials

The Three Treasures

Not everything that is faced can be changed, but nothing can be changed until it is faced.

—*James Baldwin*

1. Committing to Living with Intimacy
Wakefulness

Below the New York Zen Center for Contemplative Care there is a very enthusiastic personal trainer named Sammy, who leads a loud exercise class at the exact same time that we have our silent meditation group on Monday and Wednesday evenings and Saturday and Sunday mornings. For the last year, I've had an ongoing relationship with Sammy that consists of my constantly going downstairs and saying, "Hi, Sammy. I know you're really excited about your class, but the floor is vibrating upstairs. Can you turn the music down?" "Of course," he says. "I am so sorry." And then the next time our group meets, it happens again. Over and over again.

Recently, though, there was a night that I decided

not to go downstairs. It was partly because I was aware of my feeling of righteousness—you know, "I've gone downstairs five hundred times. I'm not going downstairs again. How many times do I have to go downstairs before he stops playing his music so loudly?" I looked like I was meditating, but actually I was sitting there stewing, getting caught up in and seduced by the righteousness of it, elevating myself above this inconsiderate person Sammy, and just generally being a jerk about it.

But then I started thinking about the times in my own apartment when I've put on music that I thought was great and cranked it up, totally unaware of the people in the apartments next to mine. Because our Zen Center is in the middle of Manhattan, we often hear ambulances, fire trucks, and other street noises, and hearing those during my meditation has always been an inspiring experience for me. Each time I hear the ambulance or fire truck, it moves me to know that people are responding to someone who is in trouble. And yet for some reason I had never approached Sammy's music in the same way; it had always felt like an intrusion. I realized that I had never actually tried sitting there and just feeling the beat of it.

This is what wakefulness is—simply looking at what it is we're doing. It means instead of being led by our conditioned, automatic, reactive way of being, we become deeply curious about what is arising in our body, our mind, and the world around us. It could be as we wait in line for the local coffee place: maybe the line is taking too long or the person ahead of us is complaining, and we're getting more irritated by the second. Wakefulness is simply noting that reactivity and returning our attention back to the feeling of our feet on the ground or the softness of our belly. It's simply seeing how quickly our mind can turn someone from a friend into an enemy, and then back into a friend again.

This is exactly where intimacy arises, and where we can change how we relate to the people around us. For me, finally feeling the beat of Sammy's music was also a way of enjoying my relationship with him, and remembering how I'm just like him,

too. For the last year, all the times I'd been "meditating," I was actually missing the opportunity to
do the work that's truly important—the realization that "Yeah. Me and you, Sammy. We're in this
together."

One thing about wakefulness is that there is no
arrival; you're never done. Wakefulness is a willingness to endlessly investigate, and that's where the
intimacy grows.

The other thing about it is that it takes
everything—true courage and commitment—and
includes everyone. The challenge may come from
someone like Sammy or someone much more difficult. I always think, for instance, of family trips
home as one of the greatest barometers for our
practice. Home for the holidays, to the people who
ignite all of your oldest, deepest reactivity. Can you
be awake and intimate with your mother or father
or brother or sister or aunt, whoever it is who is the
biggest pain in your ass and gets under your skin
the most?

I remember five years ago I was with my father at Cape Cod, where my family spent most of our summers when I was growing up. My dad and I like to take long epic walks on the beach together. We were on one of these walks, going down the shoreline, when he asked me for my advice about a particular person, someone who faces a lot of challenges, but perhaps more pertinently for me in that moment, someone who has deeply harmed me, as well as many other people.

It wasn't the first time Dad had asked me for advice about this person. In fact, he does it a lot, and historically it has made me crazy. I sense that he's not able to see this person for the way they actually are, which has made me feel unsafe in the past. So when my father asks me for advice about him, it can feel like a potential betrayal of a young part of myself who needed a protector.

There we were, on this beautiful beach, when my father asked for my advice again. And even though I knew we were repeating the same old pattern, I dived into it. I stepped into the trap we cocreate.

From zero to one hundred in a second, I was totally enraged with my dad, just pissed off and frustrated, and we got into a heated fight. I was about to say something really unkind when I stopped for a second and said, "Let's look at the ocean." That was the irony of it—here we were in this gorgeous place, going after each other's necks. After a pause and feeling my breath in my belly, I said, "I'm sorry I agreed to answer your question. I understand that you want my help. I love you so much, and I would love to help you, but this dynamic never ends up going well." Just like that, something broke open. It was extraordinary. In that moment I felt full, complete love for my father, even though one minute before I had been feeling nothing but rage.

He actually still asks me for advice about this person sometimes. These days, I pause, breathe, and say no. And it feels great. I waited a long time for him to change. I felt that because I had been the one who had been wronged, that he should be the one to alter his behavior. But actually, I was the one who needed to shift. I needed to change the dynamic in myself. I need to continuously practice being the protector for the young part of me. That's often the problem when we talk about relationships, isn't it? It's tends to go like this: "Well, when *they* change their behavior, then we're going to have a great time and a fabulous relationship." That's often the critical error. We're the ones who need to do the changing, even if it's totally terrifying.

There's an old Chinese story about carp and the origin of dragons. Carp are like salmon: they swim upstream by flinging themselves above the water. It's an intense thing to see, the golden fish throwing its body with all of its might. The myth goes that the carp transforms into a dragon, but only if it throws its whole body up the waterfall and through the dragon's gate at the end of the Yellow River. The dragon, of course, is a symbol of enlightenment— of complete wakefulness.

Sometimes— in moments like the one I had with my father—the beauty is in taking your whole body, using all your might, to just stop. Just stop. And once you've done that, truly feel what that's like. Establishing trust in that feeling of peace is what allows us to take refuge, to commit totally to wakefulness in the midst of difficult moments. To me, that's what taking refuge means: the decision that we're going to live from a different kind of ground. Not the ground of "I'm right" or the ground of "You're an asshole" but the ground of intimacy.

But until we're willing to have the courage and commitment to truly change the way we function, then "taking refuge" is just some idea. We need to be that golden carp. We might be scared, we might be afraid, and we are completely committed to waking up.

> How do you stop and experience the freshness of the moment?

> What allows you to be the golden carp?

Make your ego porous. Will is of little importance, complaining is nothing, fame is nothing. Openness, patience, receptivity, solitude is everything.

—*Rainer Maria Rilke*

2. Opening Up to Life's Trolls and Bullies
Receptivity

Being receptive is essentially being open to learning from everything. Some people hear this and are frightened. Others hear it and are excited, because they love learning—or at least they say they do. But true receptivity is a lot harder than it seems. And yet, if you can stay open to the lessons that are the hardest to learn, you can learn to swim, not drown, in the ocean of life.

For me, as a child, this feeling of being receptive was something I thirsted for—it was like I wanted to take in the whole universe.

When I was young, my mom and stepfather moved my brother and me to a very rural, very poor, very white town in the Adirondacks. We were the only Jewish family. At night the neighbors would circle our house in four-wheelers and shoot at it. Before we moved there, I was bullied at school for being gay; now I was bullied because I was Jewish. There was even a teacher who lifted me up by my hair and said, "Where are your horns, Jew?" I complained to the principal; I was crying as I told him. He said, "Well, where are the horns, Jew?" It was that kind of town.

In the midst of this hate, which we were literally surrounded by, at night I would still venture out into the forest and lie on these big mounds of moss. I would feel the moss underneath me and look up at the night sky and the stars. There was something really important about feeling the ground underneath me, the aliveness of the moss, the vast expanse of forest and the canopy of stars beyond the silhouetted trees. It was one of my favorite things to do, and I was nourished by it. It really helped.

That image of a scared young boy taking in the night sky and forest has always stayed with me as a model of receptivity: this innate capacity we have to hold both wonder and fear simultaneously. It's what is required in order to open up and allow all things and all people to teach you—to be totally receptive to the entire universe. And it's often the very worst circumstances, and the most horrendous people, that are the best teachers.

One of my greatest teachers at the moment is my troll. Trolls are very consistent. Or you might say "devoted." He or she—I don't know who the troll is, exactly—started by registering for courses on our center's website. They would always sign up using my name and then write all kinds of terrible things about me. We plugged up the website so that was no longer possible, so the troll moved on to taking out email addresses—always using my name—and emailing me. They did it from Google, and I had them shut down. Then they tried from Yahoo, then Outlook, and so on. The level of commitment has been amazing to behold. Five or six times daily, at all hours of the day and night, it comes in: a combo platter of how fat and disgustingly greasy I am accompanied by how gay and Jewish and also not a real Zen teacher.

I've been working with my Zen teacher about the troll since it all started, trying to figure out how I can possibly take them into my heart and even feel compassion toward them. Because what they're doing must not feel good to them, either. And even if their actions are unskillful and unkind, there's a person behind them who has goodness in them, underneath it all. So the troll doesn't need to be my enemy. That said, this doesn't make what this person is doing OK. It's abusive, and I've done the best I can to protect myself by reporting them to the police. Some days the incessant bullying takes a toll, and I can't help but think, "Why don't you just *stop*? It's enough." So to hold both of these truths at once—and to act in a way that honors both of them—has been a very challenging practice. It's hardcore.

There is an obscure Buddhist text that I love, called the *Sutra of the Fundamental Vows of Jizo Bodhisattva*. It tells us that we should be like the earth and let people shit and piss on us. I think of this teaching often when the troll situation threatens to take over my mind. Can I instead just be like the earth and let this person shit and piss on me? When I succeed, a little bit, I can notice that at the same time the troll is shitting and pissing on me, other people are planting flowers. I can see the true diversity of my circumstance: that I might have a troll but that I also receive many, many other beautiful things in my life, and that I can choose to keep softening and opening rather than letting my fear and discomfort constrict me into a teeny tiny space. But I'd never have learned all of this without the troll. The work of compassion and receptivity is not of any value if it doesn't include the worst life has to offer.

The Brothers Grimm story "The Water of Life" is also about a troll—another kind of troll. Perhaps.

In a kingdom far, far away, there are three princes, whose father is dying. He asks his sons, "Will you go get me the water of life, so I can be cured?" Of the three brothers, there's a really good-looking one, a really smart one, and one who is a bit simple and a little slow on the uptake—"the dumbling."

The smart brother goes out first. He's sure he'll be

able to figure out where this water of life is that will save his father. Right outside the palace, he crosses a bridge, and there's a troll living underneath it. The troll comes out, and the prince says, "Get away from me, you disgusting troll." He eventually ends up in a canyon, stuck and mired. Then the handsome brother goes out. Because he's so fabulous, he's definitely going to get the water of life! But he reaches the troll and has the same reaction as the first brother: "You disgust me, troll." And he ends up in trouble, too.

So then it's the dumbling's turn. And he's thinking to himself, *Well, I definitely don't know where the water of life is, but I'm the only one left, so I guess I've got to participate.* It's kind of beautiful—he's just going to get the water of life because that's what needs to be done. He goes out whistling along the trail, and out comes the troll. The dumbling greets him and says, "Oh, hi, who are you?" The troll is so happy. He says, "I'm the troll under the bridge. Who are *you*?" The dumbling tells him his father is dying and his brothers are gone, so now he's trying to find the water of life so his dad can be cured. And the troll says, "Oh, I can tell you where the water of life is!" And he leads the dumbling to the water of life, and the king is saved.

I love this pairing of the dumbling and the troll: these two qualities that we tend to not value. But they're the key. The troll represents the ugly and the unappreciated, and the dumbling, the model of being receptive to it: "Oh, a troll. And who are *you*?" And together they go and retrieve the water of life. That kind of hospitality toward the entire universe is a radical move. Rumi, the great Sufi poet and mystic, writes in "The Guest House," "Whatever comes to your door, invite it in." Even when it's a nasty troll.

> How can you open yourself to what is actually happening?
>
> How can you allow the dumbling and the trolls of life (and in yourself!) to teach you about compassion?

Life is very short and what we have to do
must be done in the now.

—*Audre Lorde*

3. Living Like Everything Matters
Being of Service to Others

There are so many amazing things in this world, and one of them is that the Dalai Lama is on Twitter.

"To serve others," he tweeted, "is the standard of a meaningful life."

There's a probably apocryphal story that goes like this: Someone once asked the Dalai Lama for help. "I feel so bad," they told him. "I don't feel any kind of compassion for myself." His advice? "Serve others."

I remember being in a Zen silent retreat, called *sesshin*, over twenty years ago. The beauty and the difficulty of being on sesshin is that everyone does exactly the same thing at exactly the same time. We all eat together, and rest together, and meditate together, and stand up together, and sit down together, and bow together, and . . . you get the idea.

I remember sitting there on a cushion and suddenly realizing that it wasn't what I spent most of my time evaluating—*my* practice, how *I* was doing, the state *I* was in on retreat—that mattered. What actually mattered was how in the flow with other people I was. I understood in that moment that the subtle nuances in my presence and behavior were affecting the people around me, and that this was a small-scale example of how I go through my entire life. It felt like the blinders had come off. The light in the room was dim, and yet everything seemed so bright.

For the first ten years of my meditation practice, I was so intensely self-preoccupied that there was no way I was really serving others. I was in it for me. In some ways, that can be helpful in the beginning. As Dogen (remember Dogen, my Zen inspiration?) says, "To study the Way is to study the self." We do have to take care of getting to know our own mind and our emotional patterns, so we can start seeing how we project our angels and demons onto other people. And yet, at a certain point in our practice, there comes a time when we have to take the courageous leap into realizing, "Oh, you matter, too!"

My friend Dean, who has schizophrenia and lives outside the Starbucks around the corner from the Zen Center, is one of my greatest teachers in this regard. I am always moved by his capacity to really see people. He's curious about each person and how they're doing, and he knows so much about the regulars who come to chat with him. I asked him once what that was all about, and he said, "Well, everyone matters." How many of us can really say that we function with that attitude? The default is usually "I matter, and everyone else matters inasmuch as they relate to me mattering." But the truth is that if we can just widen our perspective, we'll come to understand and experience that "I am me because of you."

This is what I mean: The other day I was sitting with a student who was wearing a very beautiful handmade brown sweater. I asked her, "Where

Wisdom

WISDOM PUBLICATIONS

Please fill out and return this card if you would like to receive
our catalogue and special offers. The postage is already paid!

NAME

ADDRESS

CITY / STATE / ZIP / COUNTRY

EMAIL

Sign up for our newsletter and special offers at wisdompubs.org

Wisdom Publications is a non-profit charitable organization.

did the sheep come from that offered their wool for your sweater?" And it became this amazing moment where we realized—oh, right, we have no idea. We go around without an appreciation for just how dependent we are on everything around us. In the case of just one sweater, its existence depends on the sheep, and the farmers who tended the sheep, and the people who knitted the wool, and on and on and on. When we can see and appreciate this panoramic view, we understand how we are affected by everything, even by things that might never cross our mind. Like dinosaurs. And cave people from forty thousand years ago. Who knows. It's incomprehensible.

Zen master Taizan Maezumi Roshi used to say: "I'm responsible, you're responsible." In the Zen tradition, there's a chant that we recite in the morning: "All evil karma ever committed by me, since of old, on account of my beginningless greed, anger, and ignorance. Now, I atone for it all." At first when I heard that verse I was like, *Uh, I don't want to be responsible for all of that.* There was a sense of burden. But with practice, taking responsibility feels joyful, and that's why the Dalai Lama gave the advice he did. Serve others.

I used to see myself as a rebel. Like I told you, I was really into the idea of an identity as an outsider, and it was a place of safety for me for a long time. It wasn't until I began learning to live by what was most meaningful to me, and beginning to play with that within myself, that I realized that I was responsible not only for myself but also for everyone else. And that, actually, it felt good; actually, it mattered.

There was one year in my life when I vowed to live by two words, which were *compassion* and *service*. It happened to be the first year that my grandmother Mimi got sick. Her kids, my dad and his sister, wanted her to move to assisted living near where they lived in Syracuse or Atlanta, respectively. Neither option appealed to her, and so she asked if I would be willing to take care of her instead.

We were sitting on a wooden bench on Ocean Parkway, and I was feeling these little inward contractions, like, "Oh my God, she's asking *me*?" We have a habit of this: of making our lives as tight and small as possible, and cutting ourselves off from others. It's heartbreaking, the isolation we are prone to falling into.

But that day on the bench, at the same time I was thinking about how taking on this responsibility might not necessarily be very convenient, I was also feeling such enormous love for her that I was able to expand outward again. And so I told her that of course I would take care of her. This whole response took a minute.

I was privileged to be able to learn that what "taking care of her" meant was incredibly ordinary. It was going to King's Highway grocery store and picking up whole milk and half a dozen eggs. Or sometimes it was accompanying her on doctor's visits, but mainly so I could make sure that we could get in and out of the car easily, which just meant telling her to hang on and then going around to her side of the car and opening her car door. It was totally simple, and totally loving.

The wonderful poet Rainer Maria Rilke once was apprenticed to Auguste Rodin, the incredible sculptor and artist. As part of his training, Rodin asked him to go to a museum and sit in front of one piece of art for a day and then go to a zoo and sit in front of one animal for a day. One of the poems that emerged from this exercise was the magnificent "Archaic Torso of Apollo," which describes an ancient Greek sculpted torso. It ends, ". . . for here there is no place / that does not see you. You must change your life."

How do we change our life? The answer is one of my favorite instructions from kindergarten: "Stop, look, and listen"—to whatever is in front of you, just like Rodin asked Rilke to do. We show up. For instance, if I'm talking to another person, and I really "stop, look, and listen," suddenly I'm seeing the quality of the person's face, the way their shoulders are placed, how they're sitting in the chair. I'm getting curious, and now everything becomes more alive. Suddenly the other person matters. And then—whoa—the kitchen chair matters, and the round wooden table matters, and the clay tile floor matters. To sit with things and really let them enter—to me, this is one of the most magnificent generosities. I think about Rilke just sitting there in the museum, so alone, not sure what he should be doing or feeling or what kind of artist he was, and then looking up at this "archaic torso of Apollo," and really beginning to receive it. Wow.

What changes when we simply pay attention and show up to life is amazing. One of our contemplative carepartners who trained with us at the center was working at a nursing home when she encountered a female resident who had been living there for seven years. She sat down in the chair next to her and introduced herself, all the while making eye contact with this lady. The lady seemed puzzled and started to cry. "You're looking at me," she said. "I am," the student said, "I'm looking at your beautiful blue eyes." The lady responded, "My family is all dead. My friends stopped coming years ago. People come in here all the time and do things to me, but no one actually sees me. No one has looked at me like that in seven years." This simple act of being present to another human being is so moving. What actually matters is just showing up to tune in to what's happening in front of you and all around you, and to know that "for here / there is no place that does not see you." This is how we are of service to others.

What does it feel like to meet everyone as a buddha?

What can you meet anew today?

I've learned that men and women who are living wholehearted lives really allow themselves to soften into joy and happiness. They allow themselves to experience it.

—*Brene Brown*

Part II Transforming Our Minds

The Pure Precepts

The first problem for all of us is not to learn,
but to unlearn.

—*Gloria Steinem*

4. Inviting Freshness through Not Knowing
Do No Evil

There's a great poem from the Third Ancestor of the Zen tradition that begins, "The Great Way is not difficult for those who don't cling to preferences."

Right—easier said than done. Usually, our preferences rule the roost. Conditioned feelings and opinions tend to determine how we behave in all of our relationships, which means that, in our every interaction, we tend to follow the same script. Rather than taking the chance to interact with the moment *as it is*, we interact with the fixed ideas that live in our heads. "Not knowing" is the dropping of all of this; instead, we completely enter the moment in front of us. In Zen we call this having "beginner's mind."

In the first ten years of my meditation practice,

I was *super* into the idea of being a meditator. I was always telling people, "Yeah, I'm a meditator, actually." "I'm off to go meditate." "Did you know I meditate?" Oh, I was so obnoxious. "You don't meditate?" I'd ask people, unprompted. "You should try it." Obviously, I was not at rest with myself and was compensating for some insecurity. And obviously, I wasn't really having beginner's mind. I was assuming I knew something that other people didn't.

In Chinese, one of the translations of the word for *suffering* is "walls in the mind." Even though I was purporting to be a meditator, I was using my practice to do exactly the opposite of what it's meant to do. I was building a wall not only between myself and other people but also between me and my own mind. Caught up in my opinions and preferences, I was creating subtle divisions, because I wasn't being honest with myself. The whole thing had a kind of odor to it. I can recall people's faces when I used to do this; it was this scrunchy look like they were smelling something bad, like, "Why don't you just leave me alone?"

The behavior was coming, in part, from a place of sweetness. There was that young enthusiastic quality of finding something new that was exciting and meaningful, and wanting to share it. But in a subtle way, I was creating evil. Wow. A big intense word and idea. Evil. Creating separation. I could have simply shared my authentic experience and left it at that: "I'm really enjoying what I'm doing. This meditation thing . . . I feel like it's changing me. It's really new, and I'm really excited." But instead I made it about the other person and my opinions about what *they* should do, and with that, I distanced myself from them as well as from my own truth.

There's a beautiful quote from the American Zen pioneer and teacher Shunryu Suzuki Roshi about beginner's mind: "In the beginner's mind, there are unlimited possibilities. In the expert's mind, there are few." In every moment, there are unlimited possibilities as to what might occur. But when we follow the same old script—for me and the meditation thing, it was a habit of mine to look to other people to validate my own feelings—there are not a lot of possibilities. It's not a fresh interaction. It's totally stale, and maybe even a little stinky.

Now, some time later, I don't feel insecure about my choice to meditate anymore (in fact, I'm not even sure if it *is* a choice anymore), and I've stopped pushing it onto other people. What's funny about this is that recently I was talking to a friend who had come to the center because he was curious about learning how to meditate. I was telling him about how I used to be that annoying meditation evangelist. He told me, "I've enjoyed watching how you behave in the world, and I've always appreciated that. That's what made me want to practice here." So it took some time, but I did end up learning my lesson about it, and when I did, that's when others finally became attracted to the idea of meditating. A key part of the practice is learning how to surrender to not being in control. Allow the unfolding.

In other words, we don't need to hang up a sign. If we can live from a mindset of "not knowing," we naturally cease from evil, and we're left free to really get into things.

I love the Japanese phrase *ichi-go ichi-e*, which means "one moment, one chance." It makes me think of dew evaporating. Have you ever seen that? Right before the sun comes up, all the dew, it's beautiful. And then—so quickly—it's gone. The opportunity to cultivate freshness, to cease from evil, is always available to us. But just for a moment . . . and then it's gone.

In the story of Cinderella, she really wanted to go to the ball, but the conditions were just not right. The interesting thing about the Cinderella story is that while there are many versions of it, there aren't any in which Cinderella complains. She keeps on meeting with obstacles, and she's sad about it, and she doesn't complain about it. Her stepfamily throws lentils in the ashes and tells her she can go if she picks up every single individual lentil in time, and she gets down and dirty and does just that. Then she gets all dressed up, and her stepsisters rip the gown to shreds. Eventually, of course, she does get to the ball, with the help of some fairy-godmother magic.

There is something about her attitude that I find really helpful. She enters the situation fully. It's a totally sad situation, so she allows herself to be totally sad about it, but she also just does the next thing she needs to do, never knowing for sure how it's all going to work out.

Most important, Cinderella doesn't go and start a war with her family. You can imagine Cinderella doing that, right, and who would blame her? In feelings of fear, insecurity, hurt, we sometimes lash out. The thing is, we've been doing that really well for thousands of years. No one needs to practice how to turn the hurtful people in our lives into enemies. The challenge is to do something new instead. How can we be like Cinderella? How do we embrace not knowing, especially in the moments where it feels completely shitty, where we might be on our knees, picking lentils out of the ashes?

My teacher's teacher's teacher, Roshi Bernie Glassman, started "bearing witness" retreats at concentration camps and other places of mass suffering. He brings people together—people from both sides of the suffering, both the perpetrators and the victims—in counsel, memorial, and contemplation at places like Bosnia and Native American reservations. In 1998, I went to one in Auschwitz-Birkenau, where family members of mine had died. In fact, in my Jewish household, I had been raised to hate anyone who contributed to the Holocaust, especially Germans and Poles. I'm serious. At my childhood dinner table it was like, "Would you like some bread and butter? And don't forget to hate the Germans and Poles, and have a little kugel with that."

So, we're sitting in a circle on the train tracks at Auschwitz. It's November. It's freezing, and in that moment I was really into "Why did we come when it's so cold?"—which is part of the point. We sat by the selection site where they would send some people to the gas chambers and some to the barracks for work. We were reading aloud the names of all the people who died there, and what we had to do was simply be with our minds.

It was excruciating for me. But the more I sat, hearing the names, being with the legacy of all that evil and feeling the sorrow of all that loss, the more I started to think about all the beings throughout the world who have been or are being killed precisely because of the walls people build between themselves, because of the differences we fabricate and the things we assume. To see that each of us is responsible for that is a real ass-kicking. Because, don't we do this every day, in our own small and subtle ways?

Dismantling these walls, made up of our opinions and preferences, is a radical move. At the Auschwitz retreat, I was able to do that in part by actually meeting German and Polish people, and listening to them, and learning to love them. One Polish woman my age and I took a long walk back into the forest behind Birkenau. I trembled as I shared how I was taught to hate Poles and Germans because my family's neighbors locked them in their barn and set it on fire—before the Nazis came. She stopped on the path. Her eyes full of tears, she took my hands and said she was there because her grandparents killed their neighbors the same way. We held each other as we sobbed and wailed.

We have the opportunity to do this on an everyday level, too. Not knowing is learning how to interrogate what we assume to be true: "I'm better than you" or "everybody should meditate" or "my stepsisters are so mean"—whatever the stories we happen to tell ourselves are. This is how we do no evil.

What are your walls, and how can you take them down?

What does it mean to see everyone as yourself?

Just practice good, do good for others, without thinking of making yourself known so that you may gain reward. Really bring benefit to others, gaining nothing for yourself.

—*Eihei Dogen Zenji*

5. Relaxing into Suffering
Do Good

So much of doing good is really just about learning how to relax in the face of whatever is in front of us.

The other day, my cousins called me up to talk about their father, Jonah, who is ninety-two and has advanced dementia. He had rallied from sepsis in the hospital and had returned to his assisted living facility. But now he had stopped eating and drinking and wouldn't take his medication. My cousins were understandably anxious and scared, and wanted me to come out to his assisted living community to give my opinion about how he was doing.

I arrived at the facility, and there he was in the bed. His breath was labored and he was staring at a random spot in the ceiling. It's a scene I've seen

many times; it's how some people look when they
are dying.

My cousins, who are so sweet and love their
father so much, were practically shouting at him,
as many people speak to the dying, in desperation.
"Dad . . . Dad! Koshin's here! Do you want us to
put on some music? DAD!" He was not responding at all, and throughout his life, he had never been
hard of hearing. My cousin turned to me and asked,
"Well, what do you think?"

I told him I thought his father was doing great—
which, of course, seemed to make my cousins
totally uncomfortable. How could I say he was
doing great? He was dying. My cousins knew that,
too, even if they hadn't yet been able to fully come to
terms with his dying to themselves in that moment.

But when I sat down and looked at Jonah, he
actually seemed quite peaceful. He didn't appear to
be in any pain; in fact, he was almost radiant. His
room was covered with beautiful symbols from his
life: emblems from his military service, awards for
his groundbreaking pharmaceutical work, photos of

him doing magic tricks and dancing with the wife he loved, and so many pictures of their kids and grand-kids. And he was surrounded by his loving family.

My cousins were used to their father being very energetic and jocular, so to them, who they were seeing in that moment was not the father they had known. It was this other father, a father who was dying, and it's not what they really wanted to see. "What should we do?" they asked me. "He's not eating. Should we feed him?"

"Let's take a moment to be quiet together," I responded. When it seemed like some of the anxiety and discomfort had dissipated from them, I asked, "Does it look like he needs to eat right now? Does he look like he needs to drink?" The answer was clear. "No," they said. I said, "I think that whatever he's doing, he's just doing that. You can talk to him at a regular level and spend some loving time with him."

To me, this is what bearing witness is: just relaxing, and settling down, and learning to be in, as Carl Jung would say, "the time of your life." When we're rushing around constantly, or when we're resistant to whatever is in front of us, we're not really doing good. Even when, like my cousins, we have the best of intentions. And as with my cousins, it's good to know what we don't know and ask for help.

Personally, I learn a lot of my life lessons at coffee bars. I'm especially friendly with Sarah, one of the baristas at my local one. I watched as a woman came in the other day and ordered her drink while scrolling through emails on her phone. When the drink came, it wasn't quite right, and she completely lost it. She was screaming at Sarah, all the while checking her emails—scrolling and swiping and tapping. After she got her drink how she wanted it and left, I said to Sarah, "How was that for you?"

"She can't help herself," Sarah answered.

"You don't take it personally?"

"She doesn't know my life," she responded. "She's not even in her *own* life."

By bearing witness, we allow ourselves to be in our own lives. We are receptive to what's happening in them. We are connected to the people around us. And from there, we can begin to do good.

Bearing witness always reminds me of the story of Odysseus and the Sirens. Odysseus is on his arduous voyage home, and he and his crew must pass the island where the Sirens live. Their song is so sweet that all the ships that sail by can't resist shipwrecking on the rocky coast of their island. Odysseus has his men plug up their ears with beeswax so they can sail past safely, but he longs to hear the song of the Sirens for himself, so he has his men tie him to the mast and leaves his ears unplugged. They come to the island, and when Odysseus hears the seductive Sirens' song, he begs and struggles to be untied. But his men only tie him more tightly.

Sometimes bearing witness is just like this: a struggle. There's something very significant about the term "bearing," because what we're witnessing is not always pretty, and learning to bear it can be painful. I think of the wonderful Blake quote: "And we are put on earth a little space / that we may learn to bear the beams of love." Sometimes the difficulty is fear of love.

In 2004 I was admitted to the hospital after complications from a hernia operation and in the most pain I had ever felt in my life. I was like a wild beast: I was sweating and thrashing around in my bed. The more I moved, the more the pain increased. I was completely under its thrall, completely blinded by it, and completely under its control. I kept trying to get in touch with my breath, but it was impossible. At the height of my agony, I remember thinking, *Just put me out my misery*.

I was so shocked by that sentence coming into my head that I was able to insert the tiniest of spaces between myself and my pain. And I was able to enter that space, where I could actually hold the pain. I could bear what I was witnessing. Suddenly, there was Chodo's handsome face; he'd been squeezing my hand the whole time. There were the other people in the room, including the elderly man lying in the hospital bed next to me, watching me carefully. In that moment, I was able to return to where I actually was, to come out of the isolation the pain had trapped me in and widen out. It wasn't until I had stopped resisting the pain that I was able to take in the love that had been around me the whole time.

This is an extreme example, but it's indicative of how *not* in our own lives we can be. Instead, we're like Odysseus on his boat, or like me in the hospital, or like the lady in the coffee shop—possessed. Where am I? What am I doing? What's happening? It's like being in traffic: one second everything is fine, and the next the car in front of us has cut us off, and before we know it we're screaming and giving the finger to some old lady who missed her turn.

Life becomes alive only when we are expansive, and we can expand only when we learn how to relax: into our seat, into our feet on the floor, into our breath and our belly. From this place of relaxation, we can bear witness to anything. This is how we do good by bearing witness.

How can you practice not responding to your own reactivity in a habitual way?

How does it feel to bear witness to your experience and not have to react in the same habitual way? How do you learn how to pause?

A human being is a part of the whole, called by us "Universe," a part limited in time and space. He experiences himself, his thoughts and feelings as something separated from the rest—a kind of optical delusion of their consciousness. The striving to free oneself from this delusion is the one issue of true religion. Not to nourish the delusion but to try to overcome it is the way to reach the attainable measure of peace of mind.

This delusion is a kind of prison for us, restricting us to our personal desires and to affection for a few persons nearest to us. Our task must be to free ourselves from this prison by widening our circles of compassion to embrace all living creatures and the whole of nature in its beauty.

—*Albert Einstein*
(possibly apocryphally)

6. Living Fearlessly by Doing Good for Others
Loving Action

We're a lot like a Macy's Thanksgiving Day Parade balloon, don't you think?

Let me explain. How often, and to how many people, do you allow your true self to come out? Who do you allow to know the whole you? For many of us, it's not a lot. Instead, we present as these big cartoon caricatures of our actual selves. We want others to perceive us in a certain way, and so we work really hard—and make others work really hard—to maintain that.

Do you see the connection to the parade balloons now? If you ever look at the faces of the people holding the ropes of these balloons, they're pretty strained. It's a great image of how we create isolation for ourselves. Here we are, floating above the crowd, careening down the street. Everybody is straining to keep our hot air balloon from drifting away into the ether, because really, living like this, we could get out of control at any moment.

What each of our balloons looks like is different. For me, my "character" looks like Yosemite Sam, the old-timey Looney Tunes character. I wanted to be thought of as funny and clever and charming, loved and adored by all, but, like Yosemite Sam, my guns were ablazing, aimed at anyone who might not think I was great and liked. Yosemite Sam was my Macy's Thanksgiving Day balloon cartoon self. I expended a lot of energy trying to project that sense of self, but the truth was that I was actually a very sad person. Most of the time I felt like I was dragging around a heavy stone, because I was terrified that someone would see just how sad I was. The result of this, of course, was that no one actually knew me, which meant that no one could truly love me, and I couldn't truly love anyone else.

When I was nineteen, in college, I was walking down the middle of a quiet street with my friend Liz.

Seemingly out of nowhere, she said, "You appear to be so happy and jokey and smart, but inside you seem so sad. I don't know who gets to know that part of you." It was such a powerful statement—it stopped me in my tracks. I felt totally startled and totally exposed, but I also knew that she was right. That's when I began to understand how isolated I had made myself.

There tends to be a contradiction between how we feel, how we *want* to feel, and our actions. We want to feel loved and loving, but instead we end up feeling isolated and alone. It's because of the gap we create between ourselves and others, which causes enormous pain. I see it time and time again working with dying people. The regrets of the sick or elderly are almost never that they weren't busy or didn't achieve enough. No—it's always "Did I love well?" "Did the people I loved know how much I loved them?" This is why the crux of doing good for others is loving action, which means to reach across the gap, without hesitation. Loving action has to begin with taking a real look at how we're actually functioning in our relationships and start acting like our true selves and not as we want others to think of us. Loving action requires discarding our Macy's Thanksgiving Day balloon.

We're often so scared to do it. But consider my experience with Liz. What I feared most—that someone would notice how sad I was—was actually the most enlivening moment. Looking back on it, I feel so blessed that she was generous enough to ask a real question, to take a real risk, to have inquired in such a loving way, "What's the deal?"—and to have really wanted to know what the answer was. Because of this experience, I was able to begin shifting my behavior, and giving up my secrecy and my fear. I learned to model her loving action. I began to learn how to ask more authentic questions of myself and those I loved.

It's important to know that sometimes loving action can just look like, "Yes, tell me."

There's another story I often tell of my dad. He was in his local supermarket, where he saw an

acquaintance in the produce aisle near the toma-
toes. He had seen this person every time he went
shopping, for decades. They would always have
the same interaction: "Hi, how are you?" "How
are you?" "Good." "Good." But there was this one
day when the pattern broke. Dad did his part: "Hi,
so-and-so, how are you?" And on *that* day, the person answered, "Do you really want to know?"

My dad paused, and took it seriously, and then
told him, "Yes." It turns out that he had just been
diagnosed with a serious illness, and his kid was in
trouble, and there was a lot of stuff going on, and
he was struggling. Dad was just there for him, in
this incredible, loving exchange. It's such a beautiful example of what's possible: how two people can
show up for each other.

I know sometimes people become stressed
about this kind of exchange, because they worry
that then they have to fix whatever the problem is.
We become afraid that now we have to take care of
everything, that we're responsible for everything.
Well, we are, but not in the way that we're afraid of.

Loving action is not about fixing. Most of the time, fixing whatever it is that needs fixing isn't within the scope of our power, anyway.

Recently, I was listening to a commercial for a texting therapy app. If you don't have time, just text some therapist somewhere. I couldn't believe it. The thing is, what tends to be the most healing in a therapeutic relationship is the relationship itself. It's not usually about the particular things the therapist says or practices they recommend, but the quality in how they are with you fearlessly, face-to-face.

This is why loving action can simply be how we are on the sidewalk or at the gym. It can be about the quality with which we look at people in the eye or how we pick up a pen or tell someone that they just dropped a glove. For me, the more attentive I am, the more soft and open I can be, the more I operate with joy, and the more I bring joy to others through loving action.

This is how to live without fear by doing good for others.

What is your balloon self like, and what are the
ways in which you keep it aloft? What are the
ways you make others work hard to maintain
your balloon self?

How can you be the loving presence you are
waiting for?

Use all you have learned in your experience
what you have learned is only as valuable
as how you put it into action.

—*Rev. Dr. James Alexander Forbes Jr.*

Part III Reorienting Our Lives
The Ten Grave Precepts

The evil that is in the world almost always comes of ignorance, and good intentions may do as much harm as malevolence if they lack understanding.

—*Albert Camus*

7. Shifting from an Attitude of Harm to One of Gratitude
Do Not Kill

A few years ago, as part of my meditation practice commitment, I would go up to Sing Sing Correctional Facility in Ossining, New York, to teach meditation and sit with some of the inmates. Sing Sing is a maximum-security facility—to put it a bit crassly, no one goes to Sing Sing for jaywalking. The guys I met were very serious practitioners, perhaps more serious than any other group I've ever been with, perhaps due to the gravity of their situation.

These guys would almost never talk about the crime that had brought them to prison, and yet they would often talk about the moment right before they committed that crime. They wouldn't put it precisely in these terms, but they would describe how in that moment they weren't in relationship with their own values or the values of the people they were about to trespass against.

One of the men had killed his best friend. The friend owed him money and wasn't paying it back. He became enraged, just totally crazy about it, and the next thing he knew he had taken out a gun and shot his friend in the face.

The thing is, we all do that. Really. Shooting your friend might be an extreme example, but we are all killers, in so many small and not-small ways. Unless you've committed to living your life like the orthodox Jains, who put gauze over their mouths so as to not swallow insects accidentally and who will only eat fruit and nuts that fall to the ground, killing is a part of life. Even if all we kill are some broccoli plants, we are always going to have to take life to continue our own life. To be able to shift yourself into an attitude of nonharming is first and foremost to realize this.

Maybe we don't want to admit that we're all killers. But we are. There is a friend of mine who I would describe as a gentle, peaceful person. She's not confrontational or prone to anger or lashing out. That is, until she got bedbugs. Believe me, she went after those things like she had been given a divine directive to end the species forever. It was a bedbug genocide. She did not stop for one second to consider the fact she was taking the lives of many beings.

Now surely, you might say, it's not the same thing to kill a bedbug as it is to kill your friend. A person is not a bedbug. But the attitude of harm that catalyzed both actions is deeply similar. It's an attitude we spend a lot of time reinforcing. How many times have we eaten a pig or cow or chicken without stopping to realize that what's in front of us was a being once, too? How much life do we endanger when we throw trash into the ocean? How about when we simply walk down the street?

It might be a tough pill to swallow, but if we spend our whole lives unaware of these smaller habits of killing, it becomes that much easier to kill when the stakes are higher, because we've done nothing but reinforce the habit that killing is not a big deal. In fact, this is exactly how genocidal dictators throughout time have been able to convince others to kill their fellow human beings en masse—by stripping the victims of their humanity and comparing them to animals. But what if the thought of causing harm to any life form was as repugnant to us as the thought of killing a friend? What kind of world would that create?

I'm not recommending that my friend should have let the bedbugs take over her apartment. And while I do think it's beneficial to look for ways to minimize our footprint of harm, I'm not interested in forcing people to follow rules about vegetarianism or any other lifestyle. Those particular choices—when to kill and when not to kill—are our own to wrestle with, and there are no specific answers. The questions matter more.

So, sometimes you do need to call an exterminator. The crux of the matter I'm talking about here is *with what attitude* we call that exterminator. Is it from a place of genocidal fury, or from an awareness of the harm we are about to engage in and an appreciation for the life we are about to end?

In the Zen tradition, before we eat, there is a chant that we recite that inspires us to consider all of the labor and sacrifice that was necessary for us to be eating that meal. It begins, "Seventy-two labors brought us this food / We should know how it comes to us." These words are medicine for our attitudes of harm. To consider *all* of the elements that are necessary for us to live is powerful and naturally moves us into gratitude for the life that surrounds us.

That gratitude can be omnipresent, even if the situation is adverse. My friend with the bedbugs, for instance, had to move from her apartment because of the infestation, and she was really upset about that. But now she has a new apartment that she likes even better and is quite happy. That doesn't mean that it was a fortunate thing that she got bedbugs, but it's interesting to think about how her experience of having the infestation would have been different if she could have maintained her relationship to her values throughout. Perhaps.

This relationship is no small thing. If we are willing to apply it vigorously to our thoughts, words, and actions, we are capable of vast change.

Dharma teacher Jack Kornfield tells an inspiring story of the Cambodian monk Maha Ghosananda. In the midst of the holocaust led by Pol Pot, even while Buddhism was under attack, Maha Ghosananda invited all those who had lost their children, grandparents, mothers, fathers, and homes to gather with him. Ten thousand people came. I often wonder what their faces were like. Around a small platform, Maha Ghosananda began the traditional chants invoking awakeness, receptivity, and community. People wept and wailed. Then this monk began chanting lines from an early text, *Dhammapada*: "Hatred never ceases hatred, but by love alone the world is healed." Over and over he chanted it until first a few people joined him, and then thousands of voices joined chanting the verse of transforming suffering into love. Instead of meeting fear, rage, and violence with the same, together they changed.

I am inspired by their courage and willingness to be loving in the midst of fear and danger. This is how to practice not killing.

When have you had to kill in the last day? What attitude did you do it with?

What life forms do you value more than others? How arbitrary are these distinctions?

How can you transform hatred into loving thoughts, words, and actions?

If you want to become full, let yourself be empty.

—*Lao Tzu*

8. Being Content with What We Have
Do Not Steal

In the book *Sapiens*, by Yuval Noah Harari, which is an account of human history from the perspective of evolutionary biology, Yuval teases out the complexity of how, basically, the *Homo sapiens* who were in Africa felt like they wanted something else, so they kept meandering into new areas of the world. I bring it up because there's something comforting about knowing that this very human desire for *more*—this feeling of not being satisfied with what we already have—has been around for at least forty thousand years.

Working with dying people, I see many houses. After people die, their houses are left behind, often filled to the brim with things that they clearly felt they needed to have, like dozens of statues of lions, thousands of books, many cans of creamed corn, and so on. I'm not talking about hoarders, either—just folks. Humans are like magpies in that way, collecting shiny objects and other things that attract them. Seeing, wanting, grabbing—it seems to be innate. Something we can work with.

I have a very dear friend who has acid reflux. Two of the biggest triggers for his acid reflux are chocolate and gluten, and he knows this. But you should see him in front of a cake counter! He practically licks the glass from so much wanting, because he loves sweets. I understand that. It might seem silly, but I get like that about new iPhones. Whenever a new one comes out, I'm overcome with impulsive thoughts to buy it immediately. I want it *now*. Luckily for me, it seems like Apple comes out with a new version of the iPhone every other week, so I've had a lot of practice with riding the bucking bronco of desire. The cycle goes like this: I read that a new one is going to come out, and then I watch the little sneak preview video they do, and then I find myself going to the store . . . just to look at them. I might as well be salivating in front of a cake counter, too.

It's been interesting to pause and see what's driving all of this, which is usually a feeling of deficiency. Some kind of lack. And if I pause long enough, I realize that I've tricked myself into believing that somehow this new phone will fill in that lack. It's not just a phone anymore; it represents so much more.

I was invited to the Hampton Classic horse show. Mercedes Benz was a sponsor, and they had the latest fully loaded Mercedes SUV out on the field. Some guy came up to the car and said—out loud—"I gotta have this car. My life is going to rock with it!" He got in the car, banged on the steering wheel, and said, "This is mine!" He handed someone a credit card and demanded, "Get me one of these, stat." It was amazing to see this in action, because it was the living embodiment of how we all get swept away in our own minds. There's nothing wrong with buying or enjoying a car, if you can afford it and all that. But thinking that some object is going to make us truly satisfied and allay our feelings of lack, longing, and dissatisfaction is nothing but a fantasy.

What would it be like to be truly content with what we have? You can understand that in regard to material things, of course, but I also mean it in regard to our life in total. What would it be like to walk down the street like that? Not imagining where you're going or where you're coming from but being content with whatever the street, the world, has to offer at exactly that moment in time.

Dogen said it would be like this: "The mind and the externals are just thus. The gate of liberation is open." What? Let me explain.

At the Zen center we have a few beautiful tea bowls made by a Japanese potter, all of which are chipped now, because people wash them and stack them in the metal rack, and they're very fragile. When I talk to our community members about not putting them in the rack, they say, "They're too delicate to use. Why do we even have them?" Suzuki

Roshi had the same problem with the teacups in his own Zen center. (It must be a Zen center epidemic.) A student complained to Suzuki about the cups. He smiled and said, "You just don't know how to handle them. You have to adjust yourself to the environment, not vice versa."

This is what Dogen was saying, too. The gate of liberation is always open. Liberation from what? Liberation from walking around in a dream, like a zombie looking for contentment outside your immediate and precious life. If only you could actually recognize and receive what is here in front of you, rather than what you *wish* were here instead. Why is that so hard? I don't know, but I do know that I certainly have a tendency to want to adjust my environment to myself, not the other way around. Instead, is it possible for us to constantly give thanks for whatever our life gives us? This is how to practice being truly content with what we have—even when it seems impossible.

One of my heroes of practicing this radical contentment is the eighteenth-century haiku master

Issa, who is a beloved poet in Japan. He has a haiku that goes "Everything I touch / with tenderness, alas, / pricks like a bramble." Essentially, "Everything I touch turns to shit." He had his reasons for saying so. His mother died when he was three, and he was raised in part by a loving grandmother, who died when he was fourteen. He was sent away from his home by his father and stepmother, not returning until he was forty-nine. He then met his wife, Kiku. Their first child died in birth. Their second died as a toddler. Then a third child died, and finally, Kiku herself. It was after their second child's death that Issa wrote probably his most famous poem: "This dewdrop world— / Is a dewdrop world, / And yet, and yet . . ."

Issa was so interested in that "and yet." In a body of work inspired by incredible suffering and melancholy, there is also that incredible sweetness of the "and yet," which pervades his writing. It's a sweetness that coexists with sorrow, and it reminds us that sweetness is always available to us, if we're willing to fully enter our life, just as it is.

What gives rise to the thought of grasping? How can you notice and catch the sensation before it turns into a thought, words, and actions?

Can you, like Issa, find sweetness within sorrow?

"Between stimulus and response is our greatest power—the freedom to choose."

—*Stephen R. Covey*

9. Encountering Ourself and Others with Respect and Dignity
Do Not Misuse Sexuality

I think most people know what's wrong with really egregious sexual offenses, especially when there is a power dynamic involved: doctors having sex with patients, teachers with students, and so on, not to mention outright assault and other crimes. But there are a lot of everyday ways we can misuse the vitality of our sexuality that don't honor it as the life-giving force it is.

In the Zen Peacemakers tradition, when we speak about this topic, we advise to go about your sexual life with the guidance to "encounter all creations with respect and dignity." It makes absolute sense. When we're in the "what we want when we want it" mindset, we're not stopping to consider whether we are treating ourselves and others with respect and dignity. We're not considering how we're affecting other people.

I remember when I was a teenager a neighboring high school principal took up with a teacher, both of whom were married with kids. And actually, both of their kids were enrolled in that same high school. The two lovers ended up running off together. I'm not sure what happened after that; maybe it was great for them. But the affair not only devastated their kids but also sent ripple effects through the whole school. Everyone felt a little off-kilter about it.

This is what can happen when we neglect the respect and dignity of others. It might be one of the reasons why we humans love to place proscriptions around sex, to lay down rules about what's allowed and what's not allowed. It's not a bad reason to do so, actually. But proscriptions can trip us up, and perhaps nowhere is that more true than in the realm of the erotic.

Shunryu Suzuki Roshi loved the phrase "not always so." It's a phrase I like to keep in mind when approaching my sexual life; it's just a way to say that treating people with respect and dignity might mean different things in different contexts. There's a provocative story often told in Zen circles that speaks to this.

There was an old woman who built a hermitage for a monk and supported him with food and money for twenty years. One day, she wanted to see how he was progressing with his spiritual practice. She sent a beautiful young woman to his hut to lie in his lap and caress his face. To these affectionate gestures, the monk responded, "A withered tree among frozen rocks; not a trace of warmth for three winters." Ouch.

The young woman left and returned to the old woman, who asked, "So, what did he do?" The young woman repeated the "withered tree" response. The old woman picked up a stick, walked over to the monk's hut, and beat him out of it. Then she burned the hut to the ground.

My students are often confused when I tell this story. Aren't monks *supposed* to be celibate? So didn't

he do the right thing in not having sex with this girl?
People don't get why the old woman becomes so
angry. Well, it's not that she thought he should be
having sex, either. It was his lack of compassion—
the coldness with which he responded to a woman
making herself vulnerable to him—that got her
going, because it showed her how little he had
learned by following the Buddhist teachings.

There's nothing wrong with rejecting someone's
advances. But you can do it with warmth, respect,
and dignity—and that doesn't usually involve sitting there as stiff as a board. (Or any mention of
cold withered trees, for that matter.) For me, this
story is a great example of where things get juicy in
regard to not misusing our sexuality: considering
what is appropriate and respectful for *this* circumstance, as opposed to laying down rules for every
circumstance. Not always so.

I have my own version of this monk's story, actually. It was my very first day as a chaplain. I had my
new monk robes on, and I was so excited to visit
with patients and share my grand Zen wisdom and

compassion with them (often a tricky part for new monks). In my head, I was going to be *so* helpful. I bet I probably even thought about how lucky they were that I was available to them. You know, I was just being a total jerk.

I waltzed into my first room, full of the light of my own awesomeness, and I heard, "Hey, sexy." I turned to the voice, and there was an elderly Puerto Rican woman lying in the bed. "Come over here, *papi*," she said. "You look so, so cute."

I totally froze. This was not what was supposed to be happening. Was this patient *flirting* with me?

I sat down in the chair, and she said, "Closer." Me, the wonderful Zen guy who was supposed to be so helpful—well, I was a total mess. I had no idea what to do with this saucy old lady. But as we began speaking, I started to understand how important it was to her that she retain a sense of her own vitality by sharing her sexuality. She wanted to reminisce about her younger days on the beach in her bikini, flirting with all the men. She was old now, and had lost her legs, and missed her former self.

It was such a significant interaction for me, because it forced me to get over my ideas of what was appropriate or correct—what offering her respect and dignity would actually look like. Being a little sexy with the gay Zen monk: that's what was healing to her in that moment. Not always so.

The word *erotic* comes from the Greek god Eros. In the myth, Eros married Psyche, a beautiful woman, but still, just a mere mortal. Supposedly, he was gorgeous, but he also wouldn't let his wife see him, and that started to bother her. (I should say that it seems to me that wanting to see your man seems fair enough, but hey.) Now, Psyche had some sisters, who were quite jealous of her marrying a god and all that, and they put the thought in her head that maybe he wouldn't let her see him because he was actually a disgusting monster. So Psyche started to believe her sisters and really freak out that maybe she was married to a monster.

She tiptoed into her husband's room when he was asleep so she could finally look at him, but as she shone her lamp on him and saw that he really was a gorgeous, magnificent god and not a monster, she accidentally spilled a drop of oil and woke him up. He felt betrayed. And after that Psyche had to go through many dangerous trials so that she could stay married to him, in order to repair the breach of trust.

Just like Psyche, when it comes to sex, sometimes we make a mess of things. The hard part is doing as Psyche did, and turning toward the mess, rather than running away from it. It might require a lot of rigor and thoughtful attention. It's not easy, and yet it's important.

I liken this to the story of the Three Little Pigs, who we all know built houses of various strength—straw, sticks, and brick—so when the wolf came to blow down their house and eat its occupants, the only pig who survived was the one who had laid a good enough foundation. How do we want to build our lives, knowing trouble will come?

For a few months, out of our apartment window, Chodo and I watched a condo building rise up brick by brick. The amount of focus the bricklayers had was intense and beautiful. Lathering the mortar, checking the placement of each brick, putting it down, smoothing it out—they had to perform every step with utmost attention, because otherwise the whole thing would fall down.

It is with this kind of care and effort that we should strive to go about encountering all creations with respect and dignity. It doesn't always mean that we're going to get it right. But we can do our best to lay a strong foundation.

How does respect function in your life? And warmth? Where do they meet, and where do they seem opposed?

How can you reflect on your relationship to your erotic life in terms of respect and dignity?

What are the messes in your life that you've turned away from?

The trouble with lying and deceiving is that their efficiency depends entirely upon a clear notion of the truth that the liar and deceiver wishes to hide.

—*Hannah Arendt*

10. Getting in Touch with and Speaking the Truth
Do Not Tell Lies

To me, lying is intimately connected with vulnerability. I believe when we lie, it's because we're afraid of exposing something about ourselves.

I have a friend who works with a writer who constantly misses deadlines. It's actually not that big of a deal, because my friend knows this about the writer, and course-corrects by giving him deadlines that are weeks prior to when my friend actually needs something turned in. The challenges arise not because of the lateness but because the writer can't seem to accept this shortcoming about himself, so he writes my friend long emails with excuses as to why he's late again—imaginative stories that my friend knows aren't true. Because of this, my friend says, she's established an opinion about this writer that has jumped from the level of "struggles with timeliness" to "pathological liar," which, as you might imagine, causes ruptures in their working relationship. How much simpler it would be for the writer to email "I'm late again" and leave it at that!

I'm sure we can all empathize with this writer, though. We all have shortcomings we'd rather not admit to ourselves, habits we'd rather hide. And lying comes from all the interference we create to not actually tell a truth that we perceive will make us vulnerable.

But our thinking about this is backward. "I think the greatest illusion we have," the activist and playwright Eve Ensler writes, "is that denial protects us." She continues, "It's a weird thing about truth; it actually protects you. What really makes you vulnerable is when you're lying, because you know you're going to get caught, even by your own mind. That you know you're a liar." When you do finally tell the truth, there's a strange relief that comes with it.

One of my students told me a story once about a man she was assisting in his dying process. His final wish was to see his daughter, from whom he was estranged. My student had to put a lot of effort into finding the daughter, because the man wasn't in touch with her at all. When she did find her, and told her the father's dying wish, the daughter said, "I don't want to see him. I hate him, and I'm glad he's dying."

My student went back to the man and told him that his daughter wouldn't come. He pleaded with her to try again. So she went back to the daughter, and this time the daughter acquiesced. "OK," she said. "I'm not going to stay long, but I'll come." My student joyfully brought the news back to the father. She was so happy that she was able to aid with such a beautiful reconciliation.

The day the daughter arrived at the hospital, my student was standing outside the door in anticipation. She saw the daughter fly into the room. As soon as she got in, my student heard her say to her father, "You're one of the most awful people I've ever known. You've caused more harm to me than anyone I've ever met. I hate your guts." And then she turned on her heel and left.

My student went into the room in a panic, apologizing. "I'm so sorry," she said to the father. "I didn't know that was going to happen." The father responded, "That's exactly what I wanted to happen. The truth is, I *was* a terrible father. She's never had the opportunity to tell me that to my face, and I know it was eating her alive." So that was his last gift to his daughter—the gift of having her truth heard, which was perhaps a relief to them both.

There are the garden-variety lies we tell (I remember when I was teaching poetry, I had a student who had three grandmothers die) but another way to think about lying is our unwillingness to examine what is really true.

For me the most challenging lie between people is the lie of omission—what we don't say. Many years ago I entered into relationship with a teacher whose intelligence, commitment to the path, and

no-nonsense outlook inspired me. Over many
years, we slowly developed an intimate relationship of trust—which was hard won, as there were
many moments of distrust and challenge for both
of us along the way. For instance, our relationship
seemed to work best when I agreed with whatever
my teacher said. I did feel that I was an apprentice,
and my role was to learn, so this felt OK at first. I
became devoted and did everything I could to support and create a container for my teacher's vision.
I joyfully did anything that was requested or that
I could intuit would be helpful. My teacher often
called me "son," which, in the beginning felt like
a reward, and I enjoyed this familiarity. I sensed,
however, this created a difficult dynamic with my
fellow peers; I experienced lots of sibling rivalry
for the position of the "number-one son." After a
while, though, feeling prepared with a solid foundation on the path, I began to assert and express
my own vision, which in the beginning was, on the
surface, well received—but I felt there was something deeply displeasing below the surface. The

more I developed my voice, the more the tension increased. This continued for six years. We never spoke about the situation directly; a lie of omission existed in the space between us. Our once flowing, meandering conversations and laughter became short and curt factual conversations, and our eye contact diminished. It seemed the more I became differentiated, the wider and wider the gap became. I don't think either of us knew how to bridge the gap, and this created distrust.

In Japanese culture there is a word, *ma*, that describes the space between things. It is what makes Japanese art, architecture, and gardens so unique. So much attention is brought to the gap, to the pause, that you can really see the stone, the scroll, the tree, the shape of a branch. Without attention to the space between, there is no true beauty and life. This is what happened between my teacher and I: the ma was neglected through omission. We had known how to relate to each other earlier, and we did not know how to relate to each other in this new place.

As stories throughout time tell, when the mentor and the student can't adapt to change and talk about it together, the relationship breaks: Baba Yaga and the adventurers, Chiron and Hercules, Pharaoh and Moses, Darth Vader and Obi Wan, and on and on. This is what happened to us: the lie of omission between us created confusion and distrust, the relationship suffered, and our once deeply held respect for each other was shattered, the bond broken. While profoundly sad for me, it doesn't discount the love, respect, and appreciation I still feel for my former teacher.

My Zen teacher, Sensei Dorothy Dai En Friedman, says, "It takes everything to be free." We have to be willing to truly be in the layers and discomfort together. With shared commitment, it is possible, and preciously rare. Both people need to be fully willing to get into the muck and learn how to be in it together. When this is possible, my experience is that a deeper intimacy and trust arises.

The Zen Peacemakers understand not-lying as listening and speaking from the heart. It's a prompt to stay connected to what is authentic for you, to ask yourself—and to be brave in hearing the answer—what you conceal about your own life. We all have those weird little pockets of concealment that we create, don't we? I've never met someone without them, anyway.

One person who exemplifies the refusal to lie to himself was the historical Buddha, which is partly what makes his story so inspiring. I'm sure you know people who went into certain careers because their parents wanted them to; "I'm a lawyer because my mom was a lawyer," and so on and so forth. The Buddha's dad was like that, too. He wanted his son to be what he (Dad) wanted him to be, instead of what he (Buddha) might want to be. He was a clan leader, kind of like a king. When the Buddha was born, his fortune was told. The oracles said that he would be either a great king, like his father, or a great spiritual leader. Well, his dad sure knew which one of those options he preferred.

He took great pains to make sure that his son was always distracted by some luxury or another and didn't let him leave the walls of the palace, so he couldn't follow a spiritual path.

Eventually the Buddha did leave the palace, and what he saw, which was essentially suffering, frailty, sickness, and death, struck him to the core. It was the Buddha's "oh, shit" moment. He could have gone back to the palace and lived out the rest of his days in pleasure, but he couldn't ignore the truth of what was in front of him. So, he walked away.

In our lives, there are often expectations put upon us by another, whether it be our parents, society, what we read in magazines, or whatever. These expectations are almost like an overlay: what our life is "supposed" to be. They have less to do with us (or reality) than with some vague external idea. And then we go about measuring ourselves against that idea. That's why what happened with the Buddha is so interesting; he encountered something within himself that felt at odds with his overlay—and used that incongruency to pivot.

To learn how to be who we are, it's essential to actually listen to what's true, instead of what we've been told is true. From this space, we can practice speaking what is actually true from our lived experience. This is the practice of not-lying.

What do you conceal about your life?

How can you see and act in accordance with what is?

How can you be more loving and brave in your relationships?

All the suffering, stress, and addiction comes from not realizing you already are what you are looking for.

—*Jon Kabat-Zinn*

11. Clearing Away the Fog
Do Not Engage with Intoxicants

There was someone I knew for many years, someone I used to go visit at her seaside home all the time. We used to meditate together, and I felt that we were very good friends. But I also felt like she was often quite aloof and disconnected, and she made a lot of choices I found erratic and strange. It wasn't until Chodo met her and spent the weekend with us that I was able to figure out why. I asked Chodo, "So, what do you think the deal is?" He immediately responded: "She's an alcoholic."

As far as I was aware I had never known an alcoholic before. I didn't know how to read the signs. So this partly explained why I was ignorant about what was really going on for so long. But it was also difficult to figure out because my friend was always careful to keep me (and, in fact, everyone in her life) at a distance, because the drinking was her priority over anything else.

This is how I understand what an intoxicant is: anything that creates distance. Between you and your relationships, but also between you and your own experience. It's anything you're using to not be where you are. Anything that you're powerless to resist turning to. And especially, anything that you're using to delude yourself into thinking everything is OK when it isn't.

We live in an age of many intoxications—drinking and drugs and pornography; credit cards and phones and endless entertainment—but an intoxicant can also be needing to have a lot to do or to be the center of attention. Anything can become an intoxicant if you can't stop yourself from turning to it.

I remember when I got my first iPhone. I couldn't stop looking at it. I was always checking it, seeing if there were any new notifications or whether there was something I could do on it that would occupy my attention. A month or two after I got it, I was on the subway, and across the aisle from me there was a mother and her baby in a stroller. The baby was reaching for her mother, extending her little face and hands. And the mother, just like all of us are wont to do, was engrossed in her phone, totally oblivious to her child. That image was so striking to me. In fact, it was heartbreaking to watch. But it was such a perfect visual of the distance we create when we live our lives intoxicated.

Nowadays, when people are out with friends, they can feel that the friends on their phone are more important than the ones in front of them. And as a Zen teacher, I hear very often about meaningful partnerships and friendships that have suffered because of phones, busyness, sex, or other drugs of choice, because we aren't able to put down our intoxicants. The alcoholic friend was not interested ultimately in putting down the booze; eventually that friendship unraveled because she wouldn't let me get to know her struggling self.

So one of the most important things we can do

in our lives is to clear out the "fog machine": put our intoxicants away and begin exploring what that feels like, so that we can begin cultivating real connections. Start practicing with the "intoxicant itch"—"Gotta check my phone," "Gotta have a drink"—and see what *that* feels like.

One of my friends, who had decided to quit drinking for a while, was just telling me the other day how hungover she was and how awful it felt. I think that's a very relatable experience. She hadn't drunk in a long time, so she just had too much, completely forgetting that those unpleasant next-day feelings are why she had stopped drinking in the first place. We forget our direct experience so easily, don't we? We forget to register how things really are. So we do the same things over and over again, expecting different results and never getting them.

That's one part of clearing out the fog machine: identifying, modulating, and/or perhaps avoiding the toxic intoxicants. The other is learning to be

OK with our own vulnerability and with the parts of life that cause us discomfort, which is easy to say but takes a lifetime to practice.

Take the mother on the subway with her baby. Perhaps her child had been asleep for the past half an hour, and she was tired and bored, and that's why she reached for her phone. That kind of thing has happened to all of us. And maybe you're asking why we would even be interested in investigating that discomfort, in getting to know what being tired and bored really feels like.

Well, it's a bit like *The Matrix*. What those guys discovered when they unplugged themselves is that some things in the real world really sucked, *and* that some things were absolutely wonderful. It's what Zen master Dogen called the "ten thousand joys and the ten thousand sorrows"—the full experience of life. When we're intoxicated, we're cut off from that full experience.

The Zen teacher Charles Tenshin Fletcher Roshi tells a great story about this. After many years of practice with his teacher Maezumi Roshi, Fletcher

Roshi walked into the middle of the garden at the Zen Center of Los Angeles, where he had walked countless times before, when he noticed, for the very first time, a bush.

That's the whole story!

It is worth sharing another story, one that my friend the poet Marie Howe shared with me: the poet William Blake, when writing about his painting of Moses and the burning bush, said the bush was not burning; Moses had just seen the bush for the first time.

For both Fletcher Roshi and Blake, seeing that bush—really seeing it—was what living life is all about: noticing what's right in front of us, and being in dynamic relationship to it. Because how can you begin to apply love and vitality to yourself and everyone around you if you aren't conscious of what's around you in the first place? That simple task can be so difficult. And it starts when we dedicate ourselves to not indulging in intoxicants.

What are the intoxicants, obvious and literal
or not, in your life that keep you from being
present?

What are you missing when you live your life
intoxicated?

How can you open your eyes and your mind to
really see what is in your life today?

Students, when you want to say something, think about it three times before you say it. Speak only if your words will benefit yourselves and others.
Do not speak if it brings no benefit.

—*Eihei Dogen Zenji*

12. Practicing Loving through Direct Communication
Do Not Talk About Others' Errors and Faults

There are many reasons why you shouldn't talk about others' errors and faults, and one of them is that it feels terrible. Both to you and to the person you are talking about.

For instance, have you ever really paid attention to what it feels like to talk shit about another person? I've been out to dinner with friends when suddenly the conversation takes a turn, and the group begins gossiping about so-and-so. I'm sure you've seen this happen in your own life or participated in something like this. The thing is, if you pay attention, you'll notice it feels awful in your body. For me personally, my chest becomes heavy;

my stomach turns. Becoming acquainted with this nauseating feeling helped me stop my own habits in this arena.

There's a famous Buddhist story that illustrates this very well. The Buddha was giving a talk in front of the whole assembly—the entire community of monks, nuns, and folks who followed the Buddha when he was alive—and a guy stood up and said in front of everybody, "You suck, Buddha. You're an idiot. You're this and that." Whatever the insults were in ancient India, he hurled them.

The Buddha just listened and waited for him to finish. When he did, the Buddha asked the man a question: "If you give someone a gift, and they don't receive it, to whom does the gift belong?" The man replied, "Well, the person giving the gift, I guess." The Buddha said, "Like that, I don't accept your gift. So to whom do the words belong?"

When our words are poisonous, they poison us, too.

And then, of course, there's the effect on the recipient. It's alarmingly easy to find examples of the poison of gossip. I remember a kid from my high school who was gay. So many stories were told about him that he tried to kill himself.

Another reason why you should avoid talking about others' errors and faults: doing so often means you are playing fast and loose with the truth. Here's a good story about that.

There was an old Hasidic rabbi who found out that someone in his community was spreading rumors about other people. He brought the guy to his house and asked him to fetch him a pillow from upstairs. The man went upstairs, and meanwhile the rabbi opened all the doors and windows and took a huge steak knife from the kitchen drawer. The man returned with his pillow. It was cold in the house since the wind blew in through all the open windows, and there was the rabbi standing in the middle of the room holding this big knife. So the guy felt pretty uneasy at this point.

The rabbi said, "Give me the pillow." The guy handed him the pillow, and the rabbi cut the feather pillow in half. The feathers were lifted by the wind and flew everywhere—out the windows, out the front door, out the back door, all over the house. The gossip stood dumbstruck. The rabbi said, "This is what you do when you spread rumors. The truth of the pillow is no longer there. What you have now is merely feathers. You've broken something."

Be careful not to confuse gossip with truth-telling, from a situation where we feel that something is not right and we have to do something about it—it can be surprisingly easy to do this. I recently had tea with a teacher who I had heard from many people was spreading rumors about another teacher. I decided that I didn't like that, and that as a good spiritual friend it was my job to tell him I didn't think what he was doing was kosher.

So we met, and I told him that as someone who cared about him, I wished he wouldn't talk shit, and the way he responded was really interesting. He said, "I feel that it's my responsibility to continue speaking about this, because I have to tell the truth about this teacher." But how does he know that what he's saying is really true? I asked him that. He responded, "I don't actually know it is true, but I have heard it as truth."

"Can't we take the high road here and stay with the precepts?" I asked.

"You have your way, and I have mine," he said. After the meeting, he unfriended me on Facebook.

For me, it's helpful to investigate whether I know—for sure—that what I'm about to say is really true from my experience before I say it. Am I communicating something from my own experience, or am I repeating something I was told? If you do this, you might come to see that a *lot* of what we assume to be true isn't. Rather than truth-telling, we're actually propagating rumors.

The medicine for the poison of talking about others' errors and faults is direct communication.

An amazing thing happened once when a man named Chris wrote a really awful review of our Zen Center. I remember reading it and thinking, *Oh, that's bizarre*, because it wasn't my experience of myself, but still, I was really interested in the critique. Somehow Chris and I were Facebook friends, although I had never met him. I wrote to him and said, "I read your review. I would love the opportunity to hear it from you in person. If you'd be willing to meet, we could have a conversation."

He agreed, and we ended up talking for over an hour. It turns out he had been deeply harmed by two spiritual teachers, one in the Catholic tradition that he grew up in and one in the Zen tradition, to whom he had given a lot of money. He had heard some things about Chodo and me that reminded him of these bad experiences, and that's what had motivated the review. We had a really wonderful discussion about how painful it is to experience abusive, unethical actions from people in whom we've placed great trust.

Over the course of the discussion, I also told him how courageous I thought he was to be willing to have a direct conversation about his concerns about me. And he thought *I* was courageous for reading a negative review and reaching out to that person with open arms. Both of us had to be willing to engage, because it takes the willingness of both parties to participate in a way we aren't used to. As human beings bumbling around this world, we're not always going to be in deep emotional attunement with each other. But that's OK, because we can come into that attunement if both people are willing to be uncomfortable, have direct conversations, and stay in relationship.

These difficult, awkward conversations are also the most valuable, because they come with the opportunity for intimacy. It doesn't mean that you have to like everything someone does. But to me it's loving to say—directly to the person—"You're driving me crazy" or "What I think you're doing is ethically wrong," or anything on the whole spectrum of troublesome behavior. Then you can both move forward together.

Consider instances when you've talked about others. What is your motivation at these times?

Have there been times when something you've said has had a clear impact—positive or negative? What about times when there might have been an impact for someone else, even if it wasn't obvious to you?

From time to time we complain about all kinds of things about other people, and we feel that we are being deceived. My father told us that these others are not living outside ourselves.

—*Taizan Maezumi Roshi*

13. Realizing Equality, Celebrating Diversity
Do Not Elevate Yourself and Blame Others

Many years ago, my partner at the time and I agreed to be monogamous, but my partner wasn't honoring this contract. In fact, she was sleeping around—a lot. I was hurt by this for obvious reasons. But this legitimate feeling of hurt was accompanied by an additional layer of pain; I felt that in this story of our relationship, my cheating partner was the terrible, horrible villain, and I was the poor, innocent victim. I mutated her into something much more awful than a person who was acting unskillfully. To my mind, she was like this ghoul creature. A nasty, cheating, ghoul creature! Feeling this way about her ate me up inside.

I was working with a Zen teacher at the time who encouraged me to stay in the relationship until

I didn't feel this way toward her anymore, which, honestly, sounded like an insane thing to do. Why would I stay with someone who was cheating on me? But I did, and I spent a while examining this corrosive feeling. What I found was that this tendency of my mind to cast myself as the victim was a much more frequent occurrence in my life than I thought it was. When I started to pay attention to it, it began cropping up everywhere—at work and in my friendships, in all kinds of ways. It was disturbing and painful to see.

I discovered that this feeling of victimhood was actually a manifestation of something that all of us do frequently. We elevate ourselves and blame others. This doesn't mean that what my partner was doing was right, or that she wasn't responsible for her actions. She was, and me too. But *I* was acting as if I were somehow better than her, like I didn't also have the capacity to make bad decisions or participate in unskillful behavior. It was actually a way to insulate myself against feeling vulnerable, and to distance myself from my actual emotions about the relationship, especially the sadness around the cheating.

Identifying as the victim is one classic way to elevate oneself and blame others. But there's a whole host of other ways, too. One of them is the most obvious one: plain and simple arrogance. Another is the need to be right. And another is the habit many people have of constantly putting themselves down, which might seem paradoxical but is actually a particularly interesting way of elevating ourselves. *I'll never be like her* or *I'm broken* or *I'm not as smart or talented.* These are all just ways of considering ourselves to be different from everyone else, giving us an excuse not to relate to others as equals.

I noticed this pernicious quality in myself and continued on in this relationship, until one sunny day I was walking down the street in Brooklyn and the thought *It's done* popped into my mind out of nowhere. That was it. Standing there on the corner in front of a deli, I knew 100 percent that I didn't want to be involved romantically with this person anymore, and that I needed to end the relationship.

Our breakup conversation was actually so clear and relieving. Because I had done all this work looking into my own emotions, I was able to treat her with respect, dignity, and love instead of hatred and anger. And although the breakup was sad, our dynamic no longer felt toxic or corrosive. I had come to terms with the fact that while I may not have made the same mistakes that my partner made, she was still a person I loved, not a ghoul creature, and I was a person too; we were equals. Hadn't I hurt others in the course of romance before? Hadn't I caused those I loved pain? Of course I had. And the leveling of the playing field allowed love to exist between us again, even as we removed each other from our daily lives.

Elevating ourselves and blaming others: in part, our brain just works this way. It functions by noting difference. The key to working with this habit is not to stop yourself from this natural process of noting difference but to figure out how to live peacefully with the beauty of diversity. How do we learn how to live with the vulnerability of realizing that the way that feels right to me isn't the way that feels right for somebody else? In Zen, they often use the number ten thousand to essentially say "unlimited." There are ten thousand different ways of life, and they're all right. Easy to say, hard to actually practice, especially since we're all socialized to identify with a particular gender, class, cultural or ethnic and racial group, whatever those may be.

The other morning I was leading a class of seminary students who were part of a religious tradition other than Zen. Somehow the question came up of whether I was gay. "Well, yes," I said. There was one particular student who visibly contracted into his seat. He looked terribly uncomfortable; his body language was closed down. I asked him, "How did what I just say impact you?" He told me he didn't want to talk about it. I pushed a bit. "Do you not want to talk about it because you're uncomfortable with how I might receive what you have to say?" "Yes," he said. I told him how important it was for all of us to hear what he had to say.

The man was a priest from a country where gay people are imprisoned or murdered, and he shared this with us. "I really struggle with homosexuality," he said. "Where I come from, it's not accepted, and it's not right."

Well, I could certainly understand that. Not about homosexuality, but I've mentioned that the way I grew up was to hate all Germans and Polish people. When I was in high school, there was a German exchange student named Elka, and I thought that maybe she was the devil. It was a funny thing for me, because I really liked her as a person and was curious about her, but at the same time, I felt, *Oh God, she's one of them.* I was confused because of how I was raised and had a difficult time having a regular relationship with her because of that.

So I really did understand what this man was saying about homosexuals. I told him that I appreciated his sharing his feelings. This uncomfortable and true exchange let everyone share about the particular group that they have difficulty with, that they were raised to believe was wrong or to be hated. For some people it was women; others talked about white, black, Hispanic, Jewish, or Asian people. No one had any trouble coming up with *something* or some group that they were raised to think was lesser or wrong.

By the end of the time with that priest I actually felt warmly connected with him. For me it was an eye-opening and freeing conversation, to see that we all have the potential to be a misogynist or a homophobe or a racist. We are all the same in that way, even though each one of us is unique.

It's actually not necessarily this diversity that creates distance between us. What creates distance are the stories we tell ourselves about others—about whole groups of people, sometimes!—that set one person above another.

With lots of effort and work, we can learn to release ourselves from clinging to our stories about what other people are, realizing instead that we are all part of "the one bright pearl," as Dogen puts it, and tasting the freedom that comes with considering everyone as equals. This doesn't mean that everyone is the same but that everyone should be treated with the same respect and dignity.

This is how we practice not elevating ourselves and blaming others.

> What are the ways, perhaps including self-blaming, that you elevate yourself?

> What is a quality you dislike in others? How does this quality live in you?

> How can you practice appreciating and enjoying others as they are?

No one has ever become poor by giving.

—*Anne Frank*

14. Reversing Withholding and Offering Generosity Instead

Do Not Be Stingy

A long time ago in Japan, a monk went to his teacher in total distress. "I have many problems," he told him. The teacher said, "OK. I can help you with all your problems." The monk was so happy and relieved. Thank goodness. Here was someone who was finally going to tell him how to fix his issues! The teacher called everyone into the meditation hall. He climbed up onto the teaching platform where the heads of the monastery gave talks to the entire monastic community and said, "Everyone, so-and-so has a problem." Then he got down from the platform and left.

Everyone's got problems. And there are times when we should really focus on our problems, but there are also times when this obsession with our

problems becomes a way of feeling special and sep-
arate. It's a kind of stinginess that operates by way
of taking ourselves out of relationships, of taking
ourselves out of the entire world.

Recently a Zen student of mine came to me
because she was struggling with meditation. Every
time she tried to sit and meditate, she couldn't,
because she was having too many thoughts. This is
a super-common anxiety with beginner meditators.
People think that meditation will make them stop
thinking, but it's the nature of the brain to think.
That's its job—to secrete thoughts, dozens and
dozens per second! But many wish that they could
sit down and not have any thoughts at all. What I
found myself saying to this person was, "Have you
considered the migration of whale sharks?"

Needless to say, she was surprised by my comment. (I was too, actually.) "No," she said. "I
haven't."

"Chodo and I were just in Mexico," I said, "and
we learned that they swim with their babies all the
way to the southern part of Argentina. Right now,

as we're talking in this room, all these giant whale sharks and their little baby whale sharks are swimming across the oceans."

Struggles are important, and our struggles need to be heard, and we can also allow our struggles to rest in the context of the whole. There's a beauty to expanding our awareness out, of realizing that so many things are all happening all at the same time. Once, when Marie Howe was teaching writing, she put it like this: don't write about what's in front of you; write and include what's behind you, what you can't see. Or here's Dogen again: "One phrase, one verse—that is the ten thousand things and one hundred grasses; one Dharma, one realization— that is all buddhas and ancestral teachers. Therefore, from the beginning of time, there has been no stinginess at all." Which is just a super-Buddhist way of saying, "Consider the workings of the entire universe." Right now, somewhere in the world, certain beings can see the sun, and somewhere else, other beings can see the moon. Opening up to this world of myriad possibilities is a generosity, because it allows you to give and receive, to participate with the world, without limit.

Many of us have a habit of withholding. Let's just think about all the ways we withhold ourselves— all the ways that we are stingy about participating with the world. I can't tell you how many people I've worked with, as a teacher and a caregiver, who have talked with me about withholding throughout their lives, in particular in relationships. We withhold sharing our love, we withhold our vulnerability, we withhold expressing what's true, we withhold our curiosity, we withhold our anger and our sadness. The list is so long.

We withhold especially when we encounter difficulty, because we become frightened of risk. I think that's what I love about fairy tales and myths and all the great stories—that the heroes didn't just stop in the face of adversity. Imagine the story of Odysseus if he had given up at the outset. One problem he faced in getting home to Ithaca is that he was shipwrecked. So he would have said, "Oh

well, I guess I can't go home—I don't have a boat."
The end.

But what are we risking when we withhold, when
we meet with resistance and pull away? We're risking never living a life of conviction, integrity, and
authenticity. We're risking losing the chance to do
good. The Buddha faced a lot of adversity as well.
There was a point after he became a great spiritual
teacher that his cousin was trying to kill him out of
jealousy and envy. The Buddha could have shut it
down right then and packed it all in: "All right, my
family is trying to murder me. This is too much."
But he didn't. And all of us who benefit from his
teachings now are thankful for that.

What about emotional stinginess? What about
when we believe our feelings that there is not
enough to go around? Is it true? I remember a story
about a Zen teacher on a packed train in Tokyo. A
young mountain of a man got on the train who
was in a rage, wildly swinging his arms, and people
squeezed into the other side if the train. The Zen
teacher stayed put and patted the seat next to him,

inviting the mountain of a man to sit. The mountain laughed at him. Again the Zen teacher patted the seat next to him. The mountain paused and slumped down next to him. The teacher began to pat his shoulder, and in the next moment guided the mountain's head to rest on his lap. The mountain began to cry, and the teacher said, "Tell me your story." The onlookers watched, in amazement. How many of us would be so generous?

I once served as chaplain of the inpatient oncology team at a Manhattan medical center. One day, I was asked to pay a visit to a woman who was "oppositional, difficult, and noncompliant." No one on the team could or wanted to deal with her. "Go see that awful woman," a clinician told me. Before entering her room, I took a moment to feel the softness of my breath. Then I entered her room. "Get out of here!" she screamed even before I could see her face. We had never met before, so I knew her verbal attack was not personal to me. What makes her so angry? I wondered. She began throwing everything she had at me: a little box of tissues, that odd kidney-shaped dish hospitals always seem to have for when patients are experiencing nausea, even the pillow behind her head. I just stood there. "What are you still doing here?" she bawled. I said, "I am curious what's making you so angry." "You are?" "Yes," I said. She asked for her pillow back, raising her head so I could tuck it behind her. I sat down next to her and asked her to tell me what she was angry about. She shared with me that she had cared for her parents for over twenty years. Her mother had Parkinson's and her father had Alzheimer's, and they had died within a few months of each other a year ago. Even amid her grief, she had felt free for the first time. Then she told me that she had just been diagnosed with stage IV ovarian cancer. I sat there taking in the enormity of her situation: "Now I understand why you are so angry and hurt." "Thank you," she said. "Not one person has shown any interest in my story since I came here. I am so grateful to tell you." Sometimes stinginess looks like not allowing people their feelings and not being curious about them.

Rumi wrote a poem called "Dervish at the Door":

A dervish knocked at a house
to ask for a piece of dry bread,
or moist, it didn't matter.

"This is not a bakery," said the owner.

"Might you have a bit of gristle then?"

"Does this look like a butchershop?"

"A little flour?"

"Do you hear a grinding stone?"

"Some water?"

"This is not a well."

Whatever the dervish asked for,
the man made some tired joke
and refused to give him anything.

Finally the dervish ran in the house,
lifted his robe, and squatted
as though to take a shit.

"Hey, hey!"

"Quiet, you sad man. A deserted place
is a fine spot to relieve oneself,
and since there's no living thing here,
or means of living, it needs fertilizing."

The dervish began his own list of questions
and answers.

"What kind of bird are you? Not a falcon,
trained for the royal hand. Not a peacock,
painted with everyone's eyes. Not a parrot,
that talks for sugar cubes. Not a nightingale,
that sings like someone in love.

Not a hoopoe bringing messages to Solomon,
or a stork that builds on a cliffside.

What exactly do you do?
You are no known species.

You haggle and make jokes
to keep what you own for yourself.

You have forgotten the One
who doesn't care about ownership,
who doesn't try to turn a profit
from every human exchange."

How do you allow other people's needs? How can you release your tightness and allow for generosity? Generosity appears when we allow for giving and receiving equally, when we meet each moment as fully and as openly as we can. Once I heard Bernie Glassman give a talk about engaged Buddhist practice and service work. Someone from the audience stood and said, "It is easy to say 'just give with loving action in the world,' but I don't have enough to give." Bernie paused for a moment and responded, "You are only thinking of what is in your pockets." From a vast view, we have lots of space and capacity. You can allow great generosity when asked to pay attention, listen, and participate.

Whenever you set out in life, you're going to encounter difficulty, awkwardness, discomfort, and pain. That's guaranteed. How can we learn to keep opening up and out in the face of it? It's the people who have the willingness to work with this resistance and to stay with what's true to them that are the people who inspire change for others.

The feeling of "Oh, I can't do that" is a kind of stinginess. This is how we practice generosity: by realizing that our life is not just for ourselves, but also for others. By participating in the entire universe—whale sharks and all.

In what ways do you foster a mind of poverty in others and yourself?

How can you live a truly open spiritual life?

Anybody can become angry—that is easy, but to be angry with the right person and to the right degree and at the right time and for the right purpose, and in the right way—that is not within everybody's power and is not easy.

—*Aristotle*

15. Allowing Anger to Flow by Not Fearing It

Do Not Harbor Anger

Anger is one of those things that almost nobody likes to cop to feeling. But there's nothing wrong with anger, actually. It's just one of a hundred emotions that pass through us at any given time. Just like happiness or sadness or anything else, the feeling itself is neutral—it comes and it goes. And in fact anger can be used very skillfully and powerfully. It's an energy that has pushed us to do some amazing things, like stopping the persecution of groups of people we see as other. So this isn't about committing to never feeling angry again. This is about seeing the problems that come when we start to harbor it.

When I was just out of college, I was working in a place where all of the employees were deeply unhappy. We collectively decided that it was the fault of our boss, and we all turned against him. Everything he did, no matter what it was or what the intention behind it was, became a new grievance for us to complain about. It was such a wacky environment, because, on the one hand, there was a certain camaraderie we felt in banding together against the "evil emperor." And, on the other hand, the more we shared in our resentments against our boss, the more toxic the work environment became for each of us, the more poisoned the dynamics became.

The issues at that organization were actually not insurmountable. Our boss really just had trouble communicating in an effective and skillful manner (like many of us), and all the problems were stemming from that simple inability, which is one that actually everyone in the office shared. But rather than paying attention to our angry feelings and figuring out how to address the root cause of our hurt feelings, we moved into a process of grudge-making that we're probably all familiar with; we created a story in our head of who our boss was and why he was doing the things he was doing, and then made all our decisions about how to behave toward him based on this story, which cast him as our own personal oppressor.

There's a Zen chant that addresses this. We say, "Do not judge by any standard." This points to the difference between acting from a place of serviceful anger and acting from a place of assigning blame or wrongdoing. Here's an example that you might find a little ridiculous: you know those reusable, environmentally friendly metal water bottles that have the twist top? Nice things, right? They're so much better than jetting through plastic water bottle after plastic water bottle. Well, you might think they're nice, but the sound of those tops unscrewing drives me up a wall. When I hear that metal scraping against metal, it makes me insane.

So, I know that about myself, and when I hear someone twisting their bottle open, I let the anger be. It would be a totally different thing if I moved from those flashes of irritation to thoughts of

"Those people who have those water bottles are so rude and annoying. I hate those people, anyway. They're always so self-righteous." It sounds a little crazy, I know. But we do this kind of thing *all the time*. Rather than noting our thoughts of anger and self-righteousness and moving on from it, we keep it close to our chest and spin a certain tale—and then trouble ensues. Locking ourselves inside a bunker made of our resentments and grudges is another form of isolating ourselves.

The other day, my Zen teacher, who is over ninety years old, was walking down the street. Someone banged into her, and she fell down on the sidewalk. And the person who hit her yelled, "You asshole!"—because this old lady had gotten in their way! It's incredible. Someone inconveniences us, we feel a flicker of anger, and then we make them into an object that we want to destroy. This is how we move from thoughts to words and then actions. And anger can be a *very* powerful destroyer. All you have to do is open the newspaper any day of the week, and you'll see what holding on to anger does. It reminds me of the TV show *Ray Donovan*. In one of the episodes, the protagonist's wife dies, and— spoiler alert—he becomes insanely angry. He ends up beating up his entire family and is arrested.

But anger can be a powerful protector, too. Usually anger is a secondary, not a primary, emotion. It comes into play when we'd like to avoid feeling something in particular. Maybe it's that we feel hurt, vulnerable, or powerless. That's when the anger comes in and we're like, "Don't mess with me." This was definitely the case for Ray Donovan. He wasn't truly angry at his family, just overwhelmingly upset about the loss of his wife, and he didn't know how to come to terms with those tender feelings.

Outside the gates of Buddhist temples in Japan, you often see these two angry-looking figures. Sometimes they're embedded in the gates themselves. They're the protectors of the tradition. The thought is that you can go inside the temple for refuge, where you can be vulnerable in seeking the truth, because outside these angry dudes—they're mostly dudes—are warding off any problems. My favorite protector of them is named Fudo Myo-o, which means "immovable one." He's always bare-chested and typically engulfed in flames and has a rope and a sword; in the mythology, he uses the sword, representing wisdom, to cut through igno-rance. Fudo Myo-o uses his fearful visage to scare people out of their unawareness and slothfulness and strike down demons. While anger and wrath hardly fit our typical understanding or imagina-tions of Zen, for me Fudo is the image of how to use anger in a skillful way. No bullshit.

I love this as a metaphor for how to work with our own anger: to use its protective energy to be able to "go inside"—to consider it a bellwether for paying attention to what is going on for us, so that we can act from a place of clear thinking rather than some made-up story. The problem is, so many of us are afraid of our own feelings that we end up going the Ray Donovan route instead.

This fear might have something to do with the mistaken belief that we *are* our feelings, as opposed to just being people *with* feelings (which we all have). People think that feeling angry means that they're an "angry person," or something like that. I know for a long time I was similarly invested in pretending that I was never angry. Anger felt like something icky that I didn't want to touch, that I wanted to stay away from. I wanted to be like My Little Pony, prancing around on sparkly rainbows. It wasn't until a very embarrassing incident during a caregiving visit that I realized just how much I was invested in this delusion.

I was at the bedside of a young woman and her husband, and she was in a lot of pain. Her loving husband kept telling her, "Oh, you're not in pain, everything is fine." It was just his way of coping with his discomfort around seeing his wife hurting, and for reasons having to do with my own history, it really pissed me off. I kept thinking, *Why can't you just let her have her experience?* The weird thing was, the angrier I got, the wider my smile became. Imagine—these two people in a hospital room going through a very hard moment, and here's this so-called spiritual caregiver sitting in the corner with a bizzaro grin on his face. It was totally inappropriate and out of touch. The woman in the bed finally asked me, "Why are you smiling?" Until that moment, I hadn't even been aware that I was.

Following that experience, I worked with my mentor on how much I was using fake cheerfulness to hide my own anger, discomfort, vulnerability, and pain. She used to make me physically hold my cheeks down when I was talking about something I was angry about, because the bizarro clown smile was that much of a habitual response. Walking down the hallway in the hospital, I'd see something I didn't like, and—ding!—the big smiley face would immediately appear. It was embarrassing and weird to learn about, and it became an extremely useful barometer for noting that I was probably trying to avoid feeling something I didn't want to feel. Over time, I came to recognize that the freaky smile was a form of aggressive anger toward the people who I experienced vulnerability with. I was like the Queen of Hearts, and instead of saying

"Off with your heads," I tried to clobber them with my smile, which was rooted in my discomfort.

For me, this is exactly where the rubber meets the road in regard to shifting our usual responses to anger. What are we doing with our own feelings? There's a saying that "the finger of practice always points to us," and I do believe that. Think for a moment about what it would be like to not blame anyone for your own feelings. What would it be like to use anger as something to move *with*, rather than hold *on* to? Rather than drinking the poison of harboring anger, we could figure out the appropriate medicine for any circumstance we find ourselves in.

When we do that, we begin to see the difference between blind aggression and great determination. Our actions move from being self-centered to being useful healing mechanisms for the moment at hand. Anger is like Shiva in that way. You know: she will mess you up, or she will bring you life. So you don't need to be afraid of it—you just need to know when to let it flow.

What are times you've become invested in
your own storyline?

In what ways do you make excuses for your
behavior?

To practice Zen means to realize one's existence moment after moment, rather than letting life unravel in regret of the past and daydreaming of the future. To "rest in the present" is a state of magical simplicity . . . out of the emptiness can come a true insight into our natural harmony with all creation.

—*Peter Muryo Matthiessen Roshi*

16. Living in Accord with Our Own Values
Do Not Speak Ill of the Three Treasures

Here in the last chapter of the book, we're back at the three treasures that this book starts with: awakening, receptivity, and community. What this last bit is about is this: don't dis them.

"Awakening," "receptivity," and "community" are basically stand-ins for what is most meaningful to us, and we "speak ill of them," as the traditional presentation of the precepts puts it, whenever we're not living in accord with our own values. Truthfully, that happens a lot.

One of the most common ways we avoid living by our values is the old "I'll do it later" excuse— the moment isn't right, or it's too hard, or all the right conditions are not present. Maybe the person you're dealing with is just too obnoxious for you to extend respect and love to them. Maybe the emotions you're feeling are just too much to bear for you to accept them. Maybe the mistake you made was just too long ago to rectify.

There's this beautiful, strange novel by the South Korean poet Ko Un called *Little Pilgrim*, which is based on one of the major Buddhist texts. The main character, Sudhana, is on a journey to meet Samantabhadra, the mythical figure of practice in the world. In the beginning of the story, he says, "I want to learn how to really walk in this world." The bodhisattva Manjushri tells him he can do that, but first he has to meet fifty-two teachers.

So he goes out on his adventure to meet these teachers, and each one is so surprising. One is a little girl; one is a ghost. One is a drunk man caked in dust, wandering in the desert. One is a person caught in a crevice so deep and dark that they'll never get out. These fifty-two teachers are supposed to represent the world. What Sudhana learns is that in order to live wisely—to live in accordance with his values—he has to see every manifestation of the world as a teacher. Nothing is left out.

This turns the "later" excuse on its head; it throws all of that out the window, and what's left is simply the intimacy of meeting a little girl, a ghost, a drunk person, a lost person. The opportunity for wisdom is always right now—and that's not just some idea. How extraordinary. And also . . . how do we do this?

My friend Frank was giving a talk at our Zen Center, and at one point he paused and said, "I wonder how many of us are actually living according to what we say is most important to us." It is a fabulous question to keep in front of us.

I have a trainer, Kenny Ulysses Grant. Kenny has been very inspiring to me, and not only in regard to exercise. First, it is delightful to just be a learner. One of my early teachers, Allen Ginsberg, used to say, if you are a poet, become the student of something else. Always be in a deep process of learning: cartography, astronomy, paleontology, or even athletics. Kenny teaches me through his example of how to be a mensch and how to stay disciplined with moving in the direction of where you want to go. Other than turning me into a gym guy (which I would have never imagined as a young gay kid), he's always making me do things that I'm sure, beforehand, are completely impossible to do.

One day we were doing box jumps, which is exactly what it sounds like: they stack big boxes in front of you, and you have to jump on them. The boxes start off low, and then Kenny keeps stacking and stacking them until they look like five feet tall. When it got to that point, I thought to myself, *I can't do that*. I manufactured a whole crazy space in my head that took less than thirty seconds to create: *Just because he's so athletic and capable, he thinks anyone can do this nonsense. He doesn't know me. He doesn't know what he's doing. Who is this guy, anyway? I should get a new trainer.* I told Kenny everything that was going through my mind.

Kenny said, "OK, Koshin. Just jump on the box."

We can live according to our values when we give our wholehearted being to them—as the golden carp leaps through the dragon's gate. Just like that.

> How much of your time do you actually spend living out the values that you say are most important to you?

> How can you jump into the moment?

Conclusion: Putting It into Action

When this day has passed, your days of life will be decreased by one.

Like fish living in a little water, what sort of comfort or tranquility can there be? Practice diligently and eagerly as though extinguishing a fire upon your head. Contemplate impermanence and do not squander your actions.

—Nenju (Zen chant for the end of a retreat)

This is our charge; how will you function in your life going forward? The historical Buddha said at the end of his life, "Don't believe anything I have said. Practice with it and see if it is true for you." So, it is time to take responsibility. It is time to not live half dead. It is time to live wholeheartedly. If not now, when?

Extend out.

Cultivate your awakened mind.

Learn from everything.

Build meaningful loving relationships.

Practice spaciousness.

Live a life that is infused with your values.

What are you waiting for?

Don't squander your life.

Appendix:
Instructions for Zen Meditation

How can you learn to be alive in the midst of your life? One way is through Zen meditation, or zazen. Unlike how we might think meditation is—relaxing, spa-like, "zenning out"—it is not like that. It is called a meditation "practice" because we never get good at it. Zen practice is about how to be free. So the work is basically to stop, look, and listen. When you get scared, uncomfortable, or restless going about your day, just soften and return to the practice.

One of the best parts about meditation is that you don't need anything but yourself to do it. You can meditate on the subway, in your office, on an airplane—anywhere! But if you have time to meditate daily at home or at a temple or church, try to find an uncluttered spot where you can sit without disturbances, and where it's not too hot and not too cold.

Zen people traditionally sit on what's called a *zabuton* (a square mat) and a *zafu* (a round cushion placed on top of the mat), but you can also create a makeshift Zen meditation area with a home cushion placed on top of a bed, yoga mat, or large pillow. You'll want to wear loose clothing so that you can cross your legs, resting your knees on the zabuton. (And also so your legs don't fall asleep!) If this position is painful for you, you can sit in a chair instead.

Sit upright so that your back lengthens along your spine, trying not to lean in any one direction. Place your right hand palm up in the middle of your legs and your left hand palm up on your right palm, so that the backs of your wrists are resting on the tops of your thighs. The tips of your thumbs should be lightly touching each other. Keep your mouth closed, placing your tongue against the roof of your mouth just behind your teeth. (This helps with all the swallowing that's about to happen!) Keep your eyes slightly open, gazing down at a forty-five-degree angle, without focusing on anything in particular. (If you close your eyes, chances are you'll be half asleep in a few minutes or less.)

If you're a beginner, you can try meditating for just five minutes at first. You might find that even five minutes is a challenge! Set a timer on your cell phone or a clock so you don't need to check the time. Then settle into your cushion and breathe quietly through your nose, without concentrating on any one thing. Thoughts will inevitably arise—*lots* of thoughts. That's OK. Don't chase after them or try to run away from them. Just let them pass by like clouds in the sky or bubbles in a stream. As a new meditator, you can also try counting your breaths—one count for the inhale and one for the exhale. Count to ten and start over at one. If you lose count before getting to ten, no problem. Start over at one. Try this practice daily for thirty years and then evaluate!

This practice is hard. Get the support you need and do zazen ideally with a teacher and community. This is a way to practice living wholeheartedly.

Acknowledgments

Deep bows to Emma Varvaloucas—with you, your talents, humor, and love of the teachings, we are here. To the fearless and wonderful team at Wisdom Publications: Daniel Aitken, Kestrel Slocombe, Laura Cunningham, and everyone else for being wonderful partners. To the Provincetown Public Library for being such a welcoming place to so many and providing the space and light to finish this offering. To Dan Harris, Martin Moran, and Pádraig Ó Tuama for being loving readers of versions of the manuscript and companions on the way. To Jim Mintz, Jyoshin Stewart, ADA James Vinocur, and Sergeant Richard Wall for their attentive care. To our White Plum lineage teachers Roshi Taizan Maezumi, Roshi Bernie Tetsugen Glassman, and Roshi Peter Muryo Matthiessen. To Robert Bly, Maddy Bragar, James Hillman, Marie Howe, Allen Ginsberg, Beverly Zabriskie, Rita Sherr, and Sherry Salman for being loving guides on the path. To my parents, who have given me life and the love of service. To Michael Stone, who encouraged me early on to write this book. To Sensei Jose Shinzan Palma for being a loving spiritual brother. There are no words to capture how nourishing our New York Zen Center for Contemplative Care sangha is—I am inspired every day by your dedication, love, and care. To the board of directors of the Zen Center for being stewards of this work; I am honored to serve with you. To my beloved Zen teacher Sensei Dorothy Dai En Friedman, who continues to teach, inspire, and embody unconditional love. And to my beautiful husband, Robert Chodo Campbell, for your radiance of being and boundless love.

About the New York Zen Center for Contemplative Care

The founding vision of New York Zen Center for Contemplative Care focuses on caring for the most vulnerable among us and designates its mission as transforming the culture of care through contemplative practice by meeting illness, aging, and death with compassion and wisdom. Zen Center is the only organization of its kind that brings together the three elements of accredited training, providing care, and Zen practice. To learn more about Zen training or contemplative care training, or to receive care, go to www.zencare.org.

About the Author

 Koshin Paley Ellison, MFA, LMSW, DMIN, is the cofounder and co–guiding teacher of the New York Zen Center for Contemplative Care, an educational non-profit organization delivering contemplative approaches to care through education, direct service, and meditation practice. He has served as the codirector of Contemplative Care Services for the Department of Integrative Medicine and as the ACPE Certified Educator for the Pain and Palliative Care Department at Mount Sinai Beth Israel Medical Center, where he also served on the Medical Ethics Committee. He is currently on the faculty of the University of Arizona Medical

School's Center for Integrative Medicine's Integrative Medicine Fellowship, and he is a visiting professor at the McGovern Center for Humanities and Ethics, of the University of Texas Health Science Center of Houston Medical School.

He is the coeditor of *Awake at the Bedside: Contemplative Teachings on Palliative and End-of-Life Care* (Wisdom Publications, 2016). His work has been featured in the *New York Times*, PBS, *Tricycle*, and others. His six years of training at the Jungian Psychoanalytic Association as well as his clinical contemplative training at both Mount Sinai Beth Israel Medical Center and New York Presbyterian Medical Center culminated in his role as an ACPE Certified Educator, chaplain, and Jungian psychotherapist. He began his formal Zen training in 1987, and he is a recognized Soto Zen teacher by the American Zen Teachers Association, White Plum Asanga, and Soto Zen Buddhist Association. He serves on the board of directors at the New York Zen Center for Contemplative Care and Barre Center for Buddhist Studies.

About the Editor

Emma Varvaloucas is the executive editor of *Tricycle: The Buddhist Review*, where she has worked with writers from across the Buddhist traditions for seven years. A student of the Tibetan Karma Kagyu and Nyingma lineages who moonlights as a professional aerialist and aerial dance instructor, she is also the editor of *Touching Ground: Devotion and Demons along the Path to Enlightenment.*

What to Read Next from Wisdom Publications

Awake at the Bedside

Contemplative Teachings on Palliative and End-of-Life Care

Edited by Koshin Paley Ellison and Matt Weingast

Foreword by His Holiness the Karmapa

"The greatest degree of inner tranquility comes from the development of love and compassion. The more we care for the happiness of others, the greater is our own sense of well-being. Cultivating a close, warmhearted feeling for others automatically puts the mind at ease. It is the ultimate source of success in life. *Awake at the Bedside* supports this development of love and compassion."—His Holiness the Dalai Lama

Kindfulness
Ajahn Brahm

"In a stroke of genius, Ajahn Brahm turns mindfulness into kindfulness, a practice that opens our hearts to others as well as to ourselves."—Toni Bernhard, author of *How to Be Sick*

Bearing the Unbearable
Love, Loss, and the Heartbreaking Path of Grief
Joanne Cacciatore
Foreword by Jeffrey Rubin, PhD

"Simultaneously heartwrenching and uplifting. Cacciatore offers practical guidance on coping with profound and life-changing grief. This book is destined to be a classic . . . [it] is simply the best book I have ever read on the process of grief."—Ira Israel, *The Huffington Post*

When the Chocolate Runs Out
Mindfulness and Happiness
Lama Thubten Yeshe

"Lively and enlightening."—*Spirituality and Practice*

Saltwater Buddha
A Surfer's Quest to Find Zen on the Sea
Jaimal Yogis

"Heartfelt, honest, and deceptively simple. It's great stuff with the words 'cult classic' stamped all over it."—Alex Wade, author of *Surf Nation*

Zen Vows for Daily Life
Robert Aitken
Foreword by Thich Nhat Hanh

A poetic classic from a major figure of American Zen.

The Poetry of Impermanence, Mindfulness, and Joy
Edited by John Brehm

"This collection would make a lovely gift for a poetry-loving or Dharma-practicing friend; it could also serve as a wonderful gateway to either topic for the uninitiated."—*Tricycle: The Buddhist Review*

About Wisdom Publications

Wisdom Publications is the leading publisher of classic and contemporary Buddhist books and practical works on mindfulness. To learn more about us or to explore our other books, please visit our website at wisdompubs.org or contact us at the address below.

Wisdom Publications
199 Elm Street
Somerville, MA 02144 USA

We are a 501(c)(3) organization, and donations in support of our mission are tax deductible.

Wisdom Publications is affiliated with the Foundation for the Preservation of the Mahayana Tradition (FPMT).